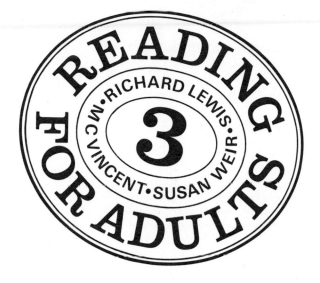

READING
FOR ADULTS
3
MC · RICHARD LEWIS · VINCENT · SUSAN WEIR

LONGMAN

LONGMAN GROUP UK LIMITED
Longman House, Burnt Mill, Harlow,
Essex CM20 2JE, England
Associated companies throughout the world

© Longman Group Limited 1977

First published 1977
Eighth impression 1988

ISBN 0-582-52792-9

Produced by Longman Singapore Publishers Pte Ltd.
Printed in Singapore.

CONTENTS

1 'A symphony in concrete'

No public building on earth looks like the Sydney Opera House: its shape is unique. In constructing it the skills of the architects, engineers and mathematicians were stretched to the limit as they struggled with problems they thought they could never solve. Many of these problems had never been faced before and probably no other single building in the world has ever used so many hours of computer time.

What makes the Sydney Opera House unique?

A great deal. It's a building of outstanding beauty; a building of enormous technical interest to architects and engineers because roofs of such size and with such bold curves have never been built before. It is the only Australian building

known outside Australia and it has already become Australia's biggest tourist attraction.

The site chosen—a finger of land pointing into the heart of Sydney Harbour—could not have been more dramatic. The Opera House stands out against towering skyscrapers, the blue water of the harbour and the greyness of the great Sydney Bridge. It is a work of art in its own right and a home for the arts that is among the best in the world.

left 'a beautiful concrete butterfly on one of the finest sites in the world', above a view of the inside

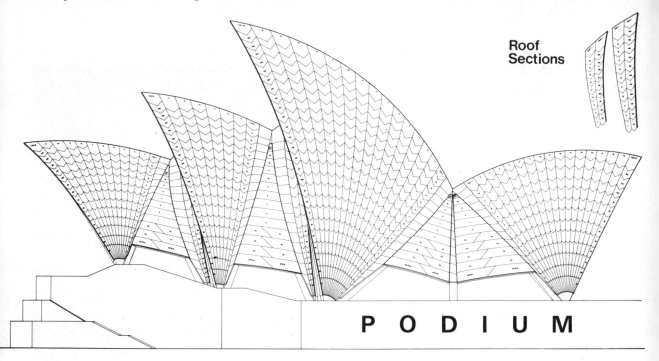

One of the architect's drawings

Roof Sections

P O D I U M

A painful birth . . .

Leading Sydney citizens often used to complain that Sydney, unlike much smaller cities in Europe and America, lacked a large modern centre for the arts. Public pressure became so great that a committee was finally appointed to look into the situation and make proposals. It considered thirty possible sites before it chose Bennelong Point. The State Government decided to find a design for an Opera House by holding a world-wide competition. The prizes were to be quite small, but the winner could expect to earn a lot more when he designed the working plans for the building and took charge of the construction. An international panel of judges received designs from more than thirty-two countries. They all agreed that first prize should go to a thirty-eight year old Dane, Jorn Utzon, who had sent in a highly imaginative, daring design of a building that looked like a beautiful concrete butterfly. The judges wrote: 'We have returned again and again to the study of these drawings; we are certain that they present an idea for an Opera House which is capable of being one of the great buildings of the world.' They nevertheless com-

mented that Utzon's drawings lacked detail. Engineers who saw them thought they went beyond the bounds of existing technology.

Even before the difficult construction work began on the roof, the engineering firm, Ove Arup and Partners, had to face unusual technical problems in building the podium. About seven hundred concrete piers had to be sunk to a depth of thirteen metres in Sydney Harbour to support the building. The company ran into so many difficulties that they had to be paid twice as much for this part of the construction as was originally agreed.

Almost six years were needed to work out a way of building the roofwork. Thousands of calculations were made using a computer. Even then Jorn Utzon was not satisfied that they had found the best answer. Working from his home in Denmark, he suddenly rang up Ove Arup in London and suggested the proposed system of building the roofs should be completely changed. Instead of pouring the concrete into the wooden shell frames when they were already in position (a difficult and extremely expensive operation) he proposed building the shells in sections and casting them in moulds on the ground. The

6

calculations would be simple if the geometry of a sphere (a perfect ball) was adopted. It has been said that this idea came to Utzon when he was peeling an orange one day. In fact many people think the building looks like a beautiful fruit or flower.

In 1965 there was an election in New South Wales. The new government thought the project was taking far too long and were also worried about the high costs. For his part Utzon had had disagreements with many engineers and government officials over methods of construction, materials and the use of subcontractors. He was also very unhappy because he said there had been a delay of certain professional fees. On February 28, 1966, he resigned. He was replaced by an architectural panel chosen by the Minister. Today, in spite of its enormous cost and troubled history, most Australians are extremely proud of their Opera House, while many architects consider it stands on the finest site of any public building constructed this century.

Above sea and sky can be seen through the enormous glass walls, right *sections of the roof being put in position*

Jorn Utzon, architect of the Sydney Opera House

Far away from Australia on the north coast of Denmark lies the famous old ship-building town of Helsingor. It is perhaps better known in the English-speaking world as Elsinore, the setting for Shakespeare's play, 'Hamlet'. Hamlet, prince of Denmark, lived and died in the castle of Elsinore. Jorn Utzon, the Danish prizewinning architect of the Sydney Opera House, used to play on the castle walls as a child, for he grew up a few miles away, near the little village of Hellebaek. The castle's dramatic position, almost at the water's edge, has had a deep and lasting influence on his work as an architect, and he was clearly aiming to create the same striking effect in his designs for the Sydney Opera House. But childhood experiences and memories have not been the only influence on Utzon's work. He has travelled widely and is particularly interested in the architecture of the ancient Mayan temples in Mexico. Many critics think that the strong horizontal lines which characterise much of Utzon's work (the Sydney Opera House podium is a perfect example) reflect a Mayan influence.

At the time of the competition Utzon was starting to become known as an architectural thinker in Europe, for he had won half a dozen Danish competitions. When, at the age of 38, he won the Sydney Opera House competition, his name became internationally known. Later, while he was in Sydney working on the Opera House plans, Utzon won another international competition for a design for a theatre in Zurich, Switzerland.

His abilities as a designer of original buildings are widely recognised. All his work is characterised by his strong creative imagination, but at the time he won the Australian competition he had had little experience of the practical difficulties of directing a project.

He moved to Sydney in 1963 after working on plans for the Opera House in Denmark and London, and was elected a Fellow of the Royal Australian Institute of Architects in 1965. However, his stay in Australia was not altogether a happy one, because of many disagreements he had with engineers and officials over the Opera House project. After many arguments and struggles Utzon came to a difficult personal decision: he resigned as the Opera House architect. He said in his formal letter of resignation to Minister Hughes, 'It is not I but the Sydney Opera House that created all the enormous difficulties.'

Two months later Utzon quietly left Australia with his wife and children and returned to his home in the woods near Hellebaek. Sadly, he even demanded that his nameboard should be taken down, so that, today, one name is missing from the lists of men and firms connected with the project—the name of the sensitive Danish architect whose originality and imagination gave birth to Australia's great Opera House.

NOTES
construct build   **construction (n)**
dramatic catching and holding the imagination by unusual appearance or effects
panel a group of persons, usually experts
technology practical science
pier one of the upright supports of a bridge or other building over water
cast pour a liquid substance into a *mould* to harden
mould container in which a liquid substance hardens into a particular shape
geometry the study of lines, circles, straight-sided figures, etc
project (a plan for) work or activity of any kind
subcontractor company that does certain work for the main building company
fee money paid for professional services
setting the background against which something is seen
horizontal level or flat

EXERCISES

Comprehension

Which of these statements are true and which false?

1 The building of the Sydney Opera House presented very few difficulties
2 It is Australia's biggest tourist attraction
3 It has a very dramatic position in the heart of Sydney
4 Utzon's original drawings were very detailed
5 Thousands of calculations were made for it using a computer
6 Jorn Utzon stayed in Denmark and worked from there
7 The same architect was in charge from start to finish
8 Utzon accepts responsibility for the building in its present form

Use of English

Part 1

Make exclamations as in the sample
Example You are impressed by the magnificent podium
Answer What a magnificent podium!
You are impressed by

1 ____the dramatic site
2 ____the daring design
3 ____the bold curves
4 ____the enormous windows
5 ____the beautiful lines
6 ____the imaginative architecture

Part 2

Use the information above to make 6 new sentences
Answer I have never seen such a magnificent podium

Part 3

Complete this passage by filling the blanks with suitable verbs from the passage.

The Sydney Opera House, which . . . fourteen years to build, . . . by Jorn Utzon. He . . . the competition that was organised by the State Government with a very daring design. When work started, the engineers . . . unusual technical problems, particularly with the roof. The idea for building the roof . . . to Jorn Utzon when he . . . an orange. Sadly he . . . from the project before it was finished and also . . . that his nameboard should be taken down.

Guided summary

Make all the changes and additions necessary to produce from the following series of words 6 correct sentences which together make a paragraph about the Sydney Opera House. Words in italics need special attention.

When/government N.S.W./*decide*/build/opera house/*hold*/competition
Designs/*receive*/many different countries/*judge*/international group/architects
Jorn Utzon/38 yrs/Dane/*win*/competition/very unusual design
Project/often/*delay*/technical/financial reasons
Jorn Utzon/*have*/disagreements/engineers/officials/so/*resign*/project/1966
All difficulties/finally/*overcome*/Opera House/*open*/public 1973

Vocabulary

Complete the following passage with a suitable form of the words in brackets.

The new Sydney Opera House is a big tourist 1 (*attract*). Some people think Utzon got the idea for this 2 (*imagine*) design from the castle of Elsinore where he played in his 3 (*child*). When building started, engineers discovered many technical 4 (*difficult*). The 5 (*construct*) of the roof was the biggest problem, until Utzon had the idea of building it in segments. Many visitors say the 6 (*drama*) curves of the roof remind them of a beautiful butterfly.

Discussion

Do you think the Sydney Opera House was worth the cost?
What's your opinion of modern architecture?

2 The population explosion

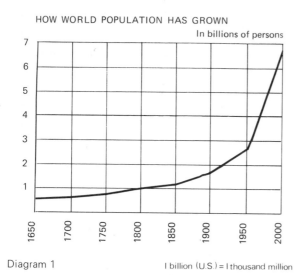

HOW WORLD POPULATION HAS GROWN

In billions of persons

Diagram 1

1 billion (U.S.) = 1 thousand million

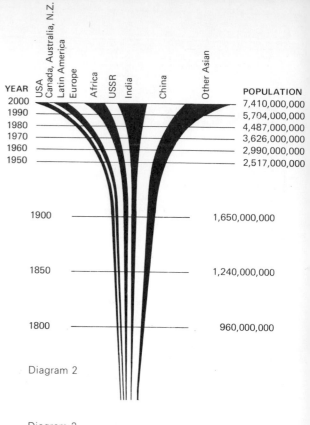

YEAR	POPULATION
2000	7,410,000,000
1990	5,704,000,000
1980	4,487,000,000
1970	3,626,000,000
1960	2,990,000,000
1950	2,517,000,000
1900	1,650,000,000
1850	1,240,000,000
1800	960,000,000

Diagram 2

Three babies born every second...

There are over 3,800 million people in the world today, and the total is increasing at the rate of more than 76 million a year. United Nations experts have calculated that it could be more than 7,000 million by the end of this century.

The population is growing more quickly in some parts of the world than others. The continents with the fastest growth rates are Latin America (2.9 per cent) and Africa (2.6 per cent). Asia comes third (2.1 per cent) but because its present population is so large it is there that by far the greatest *number* of people will be added before the end of the century.

What has caused the population explosion?

The main reason is not so much a rise in birth rates as a fall in death rates as a result of improvements in public health services and medical care. Many more babies now survive infancy, grow up and become parents, and many more adults are living into old age so that populations are being added to at both ends. In Europe and America the death rate began to fall during the Industrial Revolution. In the developing countries of Africa, Asia and Latin America the fall in death rate did not begin till much later and the birth rate has only recently begun to fall.

Diagram 3

ESTIMATED BIRTH AND DEATH RATES 1770–1970

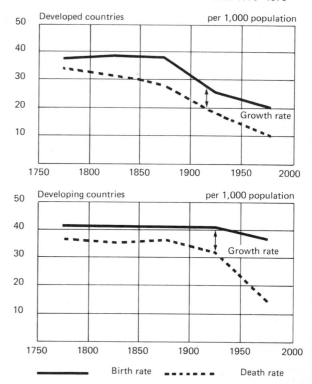

Developed countries — per 1,000 population

Growth rate

Developing countries — per 1,000 population

Growth rate

——— Birth rate   ▬ ▬ ▬ Death rate

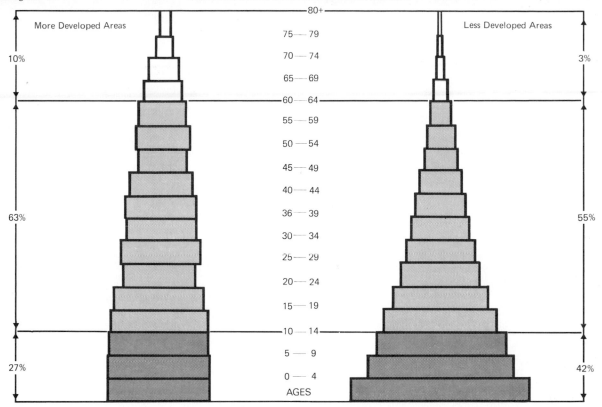

More Developed Areas

Less Developed Areas

10%   3%

63%   55%

27%   42%

80+
75 — 79
70 — 74
65 — 69
60 — 64
55 — 59
50 — 54
45 — 49
40 — 44
36 — 39
30 — 34
25 — 29
20 — 24
15 — 19
10 — 14
5 — 9
0 — 4
AGES

The problems facing the developing countries

'The rich get richer and the poor get babies...'

This sudden increase in the population of the developing countries has come at a difficult time. Even if their population had not grown so fast they would have been facing a desperate struggle to bring the standard of living of their people up to the point at which there was enough food, housing, education, medical care and employment for everyone to have a reasonable life. The poor countries are having to run faster and faster in their economic activity in order to stay in the same place, and the gap in wealth between rich and poor countries grows wider every year.

Too little food...

The most pressing problem created by the rapid increase in population is a shortage of food. More mouths have to be fed every year, and yet a high proportion of the existing population are not getting enough of the right kind of food. Over the past two years the total amount of food has decreased, and of course the total amount of food per person has decreased even more sharply.

Too many young people...

More and more of the babies born in developing countries have been surviving infancy and now nearly half the people living in those countries are under the age of 15. The adults have to work harder than ever to provide for the needs of the children, who cannot contribute to the economy until they are older. There is a shortage of schools and teachers, and there are not enough hospitals, doctors and nurses. Farming land is becoming scarce, so country people are moving to the towns and cities in the hope of finding a better standard of living. But the cities have not been able to provide housing, and the newcomers live in crowded slums. Finally, there are too few jobs and unemployment leads to further poverty.

An American in India...

'We moved slowly through the city in a taxi and entered a crowded slum district. The temperature was well over 100° and the air was thick with dust and smoke. The streets seemed alive with people. People eating, people washing, people sleeping. People visiting each other, arguing and screaming. People pushing their hands through the taxi windows, begging. People relieving themselves. People holding on to the sides of buses. People leading animals. People, people, people, people. As we drove slowly through the crowd, sounding the taxi's horn, the dust, heat, noise and cooking fires made it like a scene from Hell. Would we ever get to our hotel? All three of us were, I admit, frightened. Since that night, I've known what overpopulation feels like.'

Is there a solution?

Statistics show that rapid population growth creates problems for developing countries. So why don't people have fewer children? Statistics from the developed countries suggest that it is only when people's living standards begin to rise that birth rates begin to fall. There are good reasons for this. Poor countries cannot afford social services and old age pensions, and people's incomes are so low they have nothing to spare for savings. As a result, people look to their children to provide them with security in their old age. Having a large family can be a form of insurance. And even while they are still quite young, children can do a lot of useful jobs on a small farm. So poor people in a developing country will need to see clear signs of much better conditions ahead before they will think of having smaller families. But their conditions cannot be improved unless there *is* a reduction in the rate at which population is increasing. This will depend on a very much wider acceptance of family planning and this, in turn, will mean basic changes in attitudes.

But are not children the most important thing in life?

An African woman speaks... Mary is 39, with seven surviving children, and two grandchildren

'To us, children are the most important thing in life. When we marry, it is not above all to get a husband or wife, but to have children. I had my thirteenth birth only a few months ago, and most of my adult life I have had to care for a baby as well as do all my other work in the house and in the fields. For a long time I have wanted no more children, but I keep having them as long as I am with my husband. A nurse comes to visit our village regularly. She holds meetings for all the men and women together, to explain about family planning. Now these are well-known facts to us, but still nobody in our village practises birth control. When we sit together with the nurse, everybody seems to agree that this is the right thing to do when a family has grown big enough to give the parents security in their old age, and there are enough hands to attend to all the daily work. But when we go home, the men never talk about it. My husband and I attend every meeting, but in our home we have never talked about birth control. I desperately want to stop having more children, but this can only be done if my husband suggests it.'

It's a world problem

The rapid rise in world population is not creating problems only for the developing countries. The whole world faces the problem that raw materials are being used up at an increasing rate and food production cannot keep up with the population increase. People in the rich countries make the heaviest demands on the world's resources, its food, fuel and land, and cause the most pollution.

A baby born in the United States will use in his lifetime 30 times more of the world's resources than a baby born in India. Unless *all* the countries of the world take united action to deal with the population explosion there will be more and more people fighting for a share of less and less land, food and fuel, and the future will bring poverty, misery and war to us all.

NOTES
survive infancy live through the first five years of life
Industrial Revolution the period of great industrial change which began about 1760
desperate almost beyond hope
shortage lack; not having enough
economy system of producing and distributing the material needs of society

slum poor, dirty and heavily populated area of a city
proportion part, in relation to the whole
statistics the collection and study of facts from figures
pension regular payments to those who can no longer work
income all the money a person receives in a year
secure safe, free from anxiety   **security (n)**
pollution (of air, water etc.) being dirty and unhealthy

EXERCISES

Comprehension and discussion of the diagrams

Diagram 1
1 When did the world population begin to rise sharply?
2 What will it be at the end of this century?
3 When was it half what it is now?

Diagram 2
4 Which areas of the world have the slowest growth rates?
5 Which areas of the world have the largest populations?
6 Which areas have the fastest growth rates?

Diagram 3
7 Comment on the fall in birth and death rates in developed countries.
8 Which is falling faster in developing countries, the birth rate or the death rate?

Diagram 4
9 How has the fall in the death rate affected the age structure of the population in less developed countries?
10 What percentage of the population is of working age *a* in more developed countries? *b* in less developed countries?

Use of English

Complete this passage with a suitable form of the verb given.
World population 1 (*increase*) by 76 million a year. At this rate it 2 (*can*) be 7 billions (7,000 million) by the year 2000. Although the populations of Africa and Latin America 3 (*grow*) fastest, the greatest number of people 4 (*be born*) in Asia. In developed countries the deathrate and birthrate 5 (*start*) to fall sharply at the end of the last century and have continued to fall, but in developing countries the birth rate 6 (*not fall*) so far as sharply as the death rate.

Guided summary

Match and join the sentences in Columns A and B according to meaning and write them out as a paragraph.

Column A	*Column B*
A high percentage of the population in developing countries is below working age (so)	there is not enough work for them.
There is not enough food (Not only is … but)	the adults have to work extremely hard to provide for the young.
	many people do not eat the right kind of food.
Many people receive no medical care or education (because)	there is a shortage of schools, teachers, hospitals and doctors.
A large number have moved into the towns to find jobs (but)	

Vocabulary

Complete this paragraph with a suitable form of the words in brackets.
It has been found that the birth rate falls when there is an 1 (*improve*) in living standards. However, developing countries are not making 2 (*economy*) progress so this is not an easy 3 (*solve*). Although there has been a sharp 4 (*reduce*) in the death rate over the last fifty years, the birth rate is still high. A large family is still considered a form of 5 (*insure*) and it is difficult to get wide 6 (*accept*) of family planning.

Discussion

Do you think there really is a population problem?

3 Pets are good for you

The British have long been famous as a nation of animal-lovers, from the Queen downwards. There's a pet in nearly every family, and often the family dog or cat has a special chair near the fire, special food and a special place in the hearts of his owners. Most owners are very good to their pets; some people would say too good, like the writer of this letter to a magazine:

'My mouth watered as I imagined the lovely soup I could make from some bones in the butcher's window. There was a lot of meat on them, too. So I went in and bought some. "Certainly, one pound of bones for your dog, madam," said the butcher brightly. My next stop was at the fish shop, where I asked for some cheap fish. "For your cat?" asked the assistant. As you may have guessed, neither bones nor fish were for pets— they were for me, a pensioner. But it made me think that many animals eat better meals than people!'

Others would say that many pet owners make the mistake of treating their animals as if they were human beings:

'We have a friend who works in a Dog Parlour where they sell coats for dogs. A customer, choosing a coat, tried to describe her dog and the saleswoman suggested she bring the dog in so that they could fit him. Horrified, the customer replied that she couldn't do that as it was for the dog's birthday present and she didn't want him to see it!'

Perhaps the British *are* too good to their pets, but more interesting is a recent theory amongst psychologists that pets are very good *for* us. Dr R. writes:

'The basic meaning of "pet" is an animal we keep for emotional rather than economic reasons. A pet animal is kept as a companion, and we all need companions to keep us feeling happy. But pets offer us more than mere companionship; they invite us to love and be loved. Many owners feel their pets understand them, for animals are quick to sense anger and sorrow. Often a cat or dog can comfort us at times when human words don't help. We feel loved, too, by the way pets depend on us for a home, for food and drink. Dogs especially, look up to their owners, which makes them feel important and needed.

A pet can be something different to each member of the family, another baby to the mother, a sister or brother to an only child, a grandchild to the elderly, but for all of us pets provide pleasure and companionship. It has even been suggested that tiny pets should be sent as companions to astronauts on space ships, to help reduce the stress and loneliness of space flights.

In this Plastic Age, when most of us live in large cities, pets are particularly important for children. A pet in the family keeps people in touch with the more natural, animal world. Seeing an animal give birth brings understanding of the naturalness of childbirth, and seeing a pet die helps a child to cope with sorrow. Learning to care for a pet helps a child to grow up into a loving adult who feels responsible towards those dependent on him. Rightly we teach children to be good to their pets. They should learn, too, that pets are good for us human beings.'

P.G. Wodehouse, the famous humorous writer who died in 1975 at the age of 93, was a great dog-lover, and one of the last articles he wrote was about the pleasures, and problems, of keeping dogs as pets.

'The question of whether dogs have a sense of humour is often fiercely argued. My own opinion is that some have and some haven't. Dachshunds have, but not St Bernards or Great Danes. Apparently a dog has to be small to be fond of a joke. You never find a Great Dane trying to be a comedian.

But it is fatal to let any dog know that he is funny, for he immediately loses his head and starts overdoing it. As an example of this I would point to Rudolph, a dachshund I once owned, whose slogan was 'Anything for A Laugh.' Dachshunds are always the worst offenders in this respect because of their peculiar shape. It is only natural that when a dog finds that his mere appearance makes the viewing public laugh, he should imagine that Nature intended him to be a comedian.

I had a cottage at the time outside an English village, not far from a farm where they kept ducks, and one day the farmer called on me to say his ducks were disappearing and suspicion had fallen on my Rudolph. Why? I asked, and he said because mine was the only dog in the neighbourhood except his own Towser, and Towser had been so carefully trained that he would not touch a duck if you brought it to him with orange sauce over it.

I was very annoyed. I said he only had to gaze into Rudolph's truthful brown eyes to see how baseless were his suspicions. Had he not, I asked, heard of foxes? How much more likely that a fox was the Bad Guy in the story. He was beginning to look doubtful and seemed about to make an apology, when Rudolph, who had been listening with the greatest interest and at a certain point had left the room, came trotting in with a duck in his mouth.

Yes, dachshunds overplay their sense of humour, and I suppose other dogs have their faults, but they seem unimportant compared with their virtues.'

Doris Lessing, the novelist, describes her feelings for the pet cat she had as a little girl in southern Africa.

'I was sick that winter. It was inconvenient because my big room was due to be whitewashed. I was put in the little room at the end of the house. The house, nearly but not quite on the top of the hill, always seemed as if it might slide off into the corn fields below. This tiny room had a door, always open, and windows, always open, in spite of the windy cold of a July whose skies were an unending light clear blue. The sky, full of sunshine; the fields, sunlit. But cold, very cold. The cat, a bluish grey Persian, arrived purring on my bed, and settled down to share my sickness, my food, my pillow, my sleep. When I woke in the mornings my face turned to half-frozen sheets; the outside of the fur blanket on the bed was cold; the smell of fresh whitewash from next door was cold and clean; the wind lifting and laying the dust outside the door was cold—but in the curve of my arm, a light purring warmth, the cat, my friend.

At the back of the house a wooden tub was set into the earth, outside the bathroom, to catch the bathwater. No pipes carrying water to taps on that farm; water was fetched by ox-drawn cart when it was needed, from the well about two miles away. Through the months of the dry season the only water for the garden was the dirty bathwater. The cat fell into this tub when it was full of hot water. She screamed, was pulled out into a cold wind, washed in permanganate, for the tub was filthy, and held leaves and dust as well as soapy water, was dried and put into my bed to warm. But she grew burning hot with fever. She had pneumonia. We gave her what medicine we had in the house, but that was before antibiotics, and so she died. For a week she lay in my arm purring, purring, in a rough, trembling little voice that became weaker, then was silent; licked my hand, opened huge green eyes when I called her name and begged her to live; closed them, died, and was thrown into the deep old well—over a hundred feet deep it was—which had gone dry, because the underground water streams had changed their course one year.

That was it. Never again. And for years I matched cats in friends' houses, cats in shops, cats on farms, cats in the street, cats on walls, cats in memory, with that gentle, blue-grey purring creature which for me was the cat, the Cat, never to be replaced.

And besides, for some years my life did not include extras, unnecessaries, ornaments. Cats had no place in an existence spent always moving from place to place, room to room. A cat needs a place as much as it needs a person to make its own.

And so it was not until twenty-five years later my life had room for a cat.'

adapted from *Particularly Cats*

The great virtue of pets is surely, as these writers show, that they can make us laugh or make us cry. An animal in the family helps to keep us human.

NOTES
my mouth waters liquid forms in my mouth at the thought of tasty food
dog parlour shop giving beauty treatment to dogs
elderly (polite word for) old (people)
stress anxiety caused by pressure
cope with deal with; not be overcome by
comedian a (person) who makes people laugh
fatal very unwise (but really meaning 'causing death')
gaze look at usually for a long time
fox small dog-like wild animal that takes hens, ducks

Bad Guy criminal
trot run without effort
purr (make) the noise of a contented cat
tub round bath
permanganate medicinal substance
filthy very dirty
pneumonia dangerous disease of the lungs
antibiotics modern medicines to stop the development of disease
lick pass the tongue over

EXERCISES

Comprehension

Choose the best answer in each of the following.

1 According to the passage, the Queen *a* looks down on animals; *b* is very fond of animals; *c* has told her people to love animals; *d* is not as popular as her pets.

2 The British have special chairs near the fire for their pets because *a* an animal is a different shape from a human being; *b* they don't want to sit on the same chair; *c* they think of their pets as members of the family; *d* pets feel the cold more than humans.

3 The pensioner *a* wanted the bones and fish for her pets; *b* thought they were not good enough for her; *c* thought the food was not good enough for animals; *d* was surprised that animals ate so well.

4 The customer at the Dog Parlour thought *a* her dog would have no opinion about the coat; *b* her dog would not like the coat; *c* the coat would not suit the dog; *d* the coat should be a surprise.

5 Some psychologists think pets *a* help teach children the facts of life; *b* should be kept for economic reasons; *c* introduce children to too much suffering; *d* learn to be responsible for children.

6 Does Wodehouse think owners should encourage their pets to be amusing? Why/why not?

7 Why do you think Wodehouse believed Rudolph was innocent?

8 Why do you think Doris Lessing became so fond of the cat?

9 Why do you think she has such a clear memory of the weather and room so many years later?

10 What reasons does she give for not having another cat for 25 years?

Use of English

Example People feel loved when they look after pets.
Answer Looking after pets makes people feel loved.

Rewrite the following using the verb *make*

1 People relax when they talk to animals.
2 A person feels needed when they own a pet.
3 We laugh when we watch an amusing dog.
4 Doris Lessing felt much happier when she had the cat on her bed.
5 Children behave more responsibly when they have pets to care for.
6 Wodehouse apologised when he saw Rudolph with the dead duck.
7 Many people feel loved when they look after pets.
8 I cheered up when I got a dog for my birthday.

Complete the following using *for on to*.
The British are generally very good __ their pets. Although some people can be criticised for spending too much __ their animals, psychologists believe pets are good __ us. Pets depend __ their owners __ a home and food and dogs especially look up __ them. Pets are quick to sense anger or sorrow and often comfort people. They are kept __ emotional reasons.

Guided composition

a Choose four points in favour of pets *or* four against from the list below and write a speech introducing each point with one of these phrases:
1 The first point I should like to make is that . . .
2 It is also true . . . 3 A further point is that . . .
4 Finally I should like to remind you . . .

b Learn the speech by heart and practise saying it without looking at your notes. 1 cost very little to keep; 2 cause damage and accidents; 3 company for the elderly; 4 give and receive love; 5 spread disease; 6 make streets dirty; 7 dogs protect property; 8 help to educate children; 9 too much money spent on pets; 10 frighten small children.

Discussion

Which do you like better, Doris Lessing's or P.G. Wodehouse's story? Why?

4 A nice cup of tea

The Importance of Being Earnest
OSCAR WILDE
Act One. Abridged and adapted

Scene Algernon's flat in Half Moon Street, London, W.

Time The present. Lane has arranged afternoon tea on the table. Algernon is sitting on the sofa eating a cucumber sandwich.

Enter Lane announces

LANE Mr Ernest Worthing. *(Enter Jack. Lane goes out)*

ALGERNON How are you, my dear Ernest? What brings you up to town?

JACK Oh, pleasure, pleasure! What else should bring one anywhere? Eating as usual, I see, Algy!

ALGERNON *(stiffly)* I believe it is customary in good society to take some slight refreshment at five o'clock. Where have you been since last Thursday?

JACK *(sitting down on the sofa)* Oh! in the country.

ALGERNON What on earth do you do there?

JACK *(pulling off his gloves)* When one is in town one amuses oneself. When one is in the country one amuses other people.

ALGERNON How immensely you must amuse them! *(Goes over and takes a sandwich)* By the way, Shropshire is your county, is it not?

JACK Eh? Shropshire? Yes, of course. Hello! Why all these cups? Why cucumber sandwiches? Who is coming to tea?

ALGERNON Oh, merely Aunt Augusta and Gwendolen.

JACK How perfectly delightful!

ALGERNON Yes, that is all very well; but I am afraid Aunt Augusta won't quite approve of your being here.

JACK May I ask why?

ALGERNON My dear fellow, the way you flirt with Gwendolen is perfectly disgraceful. It is almost as bad as the way Gwendolen flirts with you.

JACK I am in love with Gwendolen. I have come up to town expressly to propose to her.

ALGERNON I thought you had come up for pleasure...I call that business.

JACK How utterly unromantic you are! *(puts out his hand to take a sandwich. Algernon at once interferes.)*

ALGERNON Please don't touch the cucumber sandwiches. They are ordered specially for Aunt Augusta. *(Takes one and eats it.)*

JACK Well, you have been eating them all the time.

ALGERNON That is quite a different matter. She is my aunt. *(Takes plate from below)* Have some bread and butter. The bread and butter is for Gwendolen. Gwendolen absolutely *loves* bread and butter.

JACK And very good bread and butter it is too.

10 minutes later

Enter Lane

LANE Lady Bracknell and Miss Fairfax.

LADY BRACKNELL Good afternoon, dear Algernon. I hope you are behaving very well.

ALGERNON I'm feeling very well, Aunt Augusta.

LADY BRACKNELL That's not quite the same thing. In fact the two things rarely go together. I'm sorry if we are a little late, Algernon, but I had to call on dear Lady Harbury. I hadn't been there since her poor husband's death. I never saw a woman so changed; she looks quite twenty years younger. And now I'll have a cup of tea, and one of those nice cucumber sandwiches you promised me.

ALGERNON Certainly, Aunt Augusta. *(Goes over to the tea-table. Picking up empty plate in*

Above *tea pickers*, above right *an old advertisement for tea*, below right *dumping tea chests into the sea at the Boston Tea Party*

horror.) Good heavens! Lane! Why are there no cucumber sandwiches? I ordered them specially!

LANE *(gravely)* There were no cucumbers in the market this morning, sir. I went down twice.

ALGERNON No cucumbers?

LANE No sir. Not even for ready money.

ALGERNON That will do, Lane, thank you.

LANE Thank you sir. *(Goes out)*

Algernon had ordered tea for his guests because, as he said to Jack, 'It is customary in good society to take some slight refreshment at five o'clock.' In fact, the English custom of afternoon tea, it is said, goes back to the late eighteenth century, when Anne, wife of the 7th Duke of Bedford, decided that she suffered from 'a sinking feeling' around 5 pm and needed tea and cakes to bring back her strength. Before long, complaints were heard that 'the labourers lose time to come and go to the tea-table and farmers' servants even demand tea for their breakfast'. Tea had arrived.

Fashionable Tea Rooms were opened for high society, and soon tea became the national drink of all classes.

Today the British drink more tea than any other nation—an average of 4 kilos a head per annum, or 1650 cups of tea a year. They drink it in bed in the morning, round the fire on winter afternoons and out in the garden on sunny summer days. In times of trouble the kettle is quickly put on, the tea is made and comforting cups of the warm brown liquid are passed round.

Tea has even played its part in wars. When George III of England tried to make the American colonists pay import duty on tea, a group of Americans disguised as Red Indians dumped 342 chests of tea into the sea in Boston Harbour— the Boston Tea Party which led to the War of Independence. In another war the Duke of Wellington sensibly had a cup of tea before starting the Battle of Waterloo, 'to clear my head'. In peace time official approval of the national drink came from the Victorian Prime Minister, Gladstone, who remarked:

'If you are cold, tea will warm you, if you are heated it will cool you, if you are depressed it will cheer you, if you are excited it will calm you.'

What exactly is tea? Basically it is a drink made from the dried leaves of a plant that only grows in hot countries. The British first heard of tea in 1598, and first tasted it in about 1650.

For nearly two centuries all tea was imported from China, until, in 1823, a tea plant was found growing naturally in Assam in India. Sixteen years later the first eight chests of Indian tea were sold in London, and today, London's tea markets deal in tea from India, Sri Lanka (Ceylon), and Africa more than from China. But wherever the tea comes from, the rules for making a 'nice tup of tea' are the same:

1 USE good tea....buy the best you can afford

2 STORAGE....store tea in an airtight container away from strong SMELLS

3 Use freshly drawn, freshly boiled water that has just reached boiling point

4 WARM the POT teapots should always be warmed before making the tea...

5 The SHORT pour....water should reach the tea LEAVES as near boiling point as possible....

6 therefore take the tea pot to the KETTLE and NOT the kettle to the tea pot. tea should

be BREWED not stewed. Brew the TEA for three to four minutes and stir....then serve with milk or lemon & sugar

7 if desired...

In Britain tea is the drink that cheers—and that is cheap. But there's a darker side to the 'nice cup of tea'. Life is far from cheerful for many of those who produce tea in other parts of the world. Many workers on tea estates suffer from poverty and poor food, and there is a high infant death-rate. A male labourer's wages for a day—a

mere 36 pence—is equal to the cost of a pound of tea to an Englishman, and that should make about two hundred cups of tea! In 1784 tea cost one shilling and sixpence a pound in England (£20 in today's money). Before long Britain's national drink may be nearly as expensive again.

NOTES

cucumber long, cool-tasting green vegetable
flirt playfully pretend to love
expressly with the intention of
disgraceful shameless
utterly completely
(un) romantic dealing with love
import duty tax on goods coming into the country

disguise change the appearance of (oneself) in order to deceive
depressed unhappy
brew put (something) into boiling water and leave it without any more heating
stew cook something in water
estate large area of land used for a special purpose (houses, factories etc.)

EXERCISES

Comprehension

Choose the best answer in each of the following.
1 Jack *a* is surprised that Algernon is eating; *b* tells Algernon not to eat; *c* expects Algernon to be eating; *d* does not want to eat.
2 Algernon *a* wants Jack to stay for tea; *b* thinks Jack should leave soon; *c* wants Jack to talk to Aunt Augusta; *d* wants Jack to talk to Gwendolyn.
3 Jack has come up to town *a* to see Algernon; *b* to propose to Gwendolyn; *c* on business; *d* to amuse his friends.
4 Lady Bracknall hopes Algernon *a* is feeling better; *b* has improved his behaviour; *c* is being good; *d* is both feeling and behaving well.
5 Algernon *a* is surprised there are no cucumber sandwiches; *b* pretends he is surprised there are no cucumber sandwiches; *c* thinks Jack has eaten the cucumber sandwiches; *d* thinks Lane has eaten the cucumber sandwiches.
6 There are no sandwiches because *a* Lane forgot to make them; *b* Jack has eaten them; *c* Lane could not get any cucumbers; *d* Algernon has eaten them.

Guided composition

a Lane made a good cup of tea for the guests. Using the information below, describe what he did. (Linking words are suggested.)

Making tea

get kettle	*First*
fill kettle	
put kettle on gas	*and*
light gas	*After*
get teapot and tea	
water boils	*When*
warm pot	
empty pot	*and then*
put in tea	*Next*
put in water	
get cup, milk, sugar	*Finally*

b Make similar lists for making coffee and boiling an egg, and then describe what you did.

Use of English

Rewrite the following sentences beginning with the words in brackets. A = Algernon
1 Algernon: Where have you been since last Thursday, Jack? (A wanted to know)
2 Algernon: It is customary in good society to take some refreshment at 5 pm, Jack. (A reminded)
3 Algernon: Have some bread and butter. (A offered)
4 Algernon: I'm feeling very well, Aunt Augusta. (A replied)
5 Lady B: I'm sorry if we are a little late. (Lady B apologised)
6 Algernon: Please don't touch the cucumber sandwiches. (A asked)
7 Lady B: And now I'll have a cup of tea. (Lady B asked)
8 Algernon: Why are there no cucumber sandwiches? (A complained)

Discussion

Which is your favourite drink and why?

5 There's money in time

Our series on 'Antiques for Everyone' continues with a look at clocks.

How should one invest a sum of money in these days of inflation? Left in a bank it will barely keep its value, however high the interest rate. Only a brave man, or a very rich one, dares to buy and sell on the Stock Market. And it's no good putting it in a tin under the bed. Wise investment is the art of making your money increase with the passing of time, and today it seems that one of the best ways to protect your savings and even increase your wealth is to buy beautiful objects from the past. In previous articles we've discussed Persian rugs, furniture and silver. This month I'm going to offer you some advice on collecting clocks, which I personally consider are amongst the most interesting of antiques.

I sometimes wonder what a being from another planet might report back about our way of life. 'The planet Earth is ruled by a mysterious creature that sits or stands in a room and makes a strange ticking sound. It has a face with twelve black marks on it, and two hands, by which it signals its orders. Men can do nothing without its permission, and it fastens its young round people's wrists so that everywhere men go they are still under its control. When it is disobeyed it makes a deafening noise—particularly in the early morning. It has even been seen to beat the top of its head with two little drumsticks. This creature is the real master of Earth and men are its slaves.'

Whether or not we are slaves of time today depends on our culture and personality, but it is believed that many years ago kings kept special slaves to tell the time. Certain men were very clever at measuring the time of day according to the beating of their own hearts. They were made to stand in a fixed place and every hour or so would shout out the time. This ability seemed to run in families, for when a human timekeeper died his son would usually take over his job. So it seems that the first clocks were human beings.

However, men quickly found more convenient and reliable ways of telling the time. They learned to use the shadows cast by the sun and invented the sundial, still to be seen in the gardens of many stately homes. They marked the hours on candles, used sand in hour-glasses, and invented water-clocks. There's a fourteenth-century Chinese water-clock in London's Science Museum which still works. Indeed, any serious student of antiques should spend as much time as possible visiting palaces, stately homes and museums to see some of the finest examples of clocks from the past.

You could pay as much as £30,000 for the work of a master maker such as Tompion, but one of the joys of collecting clocks is that it's still possible to find quite cheap ones for your own home. After all, if you're going to be ruled by time why not invest in an antique clock and perhaps make a future profit? Here are some types to look out for, but be sure you go to a reliable dealer.

Right *a sixteenth century sundial in Cambridge*

Grandfather clocks

Why 'grandfather' clock? Well, these clocks were passed down through the family and so were always thought of as 'grandfather's clock'. But the first domestic timepieces, the grandfathers of the clock family, were lantern clocks, which were hung from a nail on the wall. Unfortunately dust got into the works, and even worse, children and kittens used to swing from the weights and the pendulum. So first the face and works, and then the weights and the pendulum were protected by wooden cases. Before long the clock was nearly all case and was stood on the floor and called, not surprisingly, a long-case clock. These 'grandfather' clocks were very expensive, made as they were from fine woods, often beautifully carved or inlaid (as in the picture) with ivory. Famous makers of this period included Thomas Tompion, John Harrison and Edward East, but don't get too excited if you find that the clock Grandma left you has one of these names on the back. Before you start jumping up and down shouting, 'We're rich, we're rich,' remember that plenty of people before the twentieth century had the idea of making cheap copies of famous originals and 'borrowing' the names of their betters. And don't forget that the first chiming mechanism wasn't introduced until 1696, so a chiming clock, however charming it sounds, will date from the eighteenth century. A genuine late seventeenth century grandfather clock made by East (similar to the one in the picture) sold recently for just under £20,000.

Wall clocks

When Pitt, the British Prime Minister, put a tax on clocks in 1797 people stopped buying domestic clocks and relied instead on large wall clocks hung in public places for all to see. Many such large clocks are still known today as Act of Parliament clocks. Gradually wall clocks reduced in size and you may be able to pick up quite a neat little one

for about £50. The cheapest at £20 are some American wall clocks but they have by far the best story. A certain Mr Chauncey Jerome of Connecticut began mass-producing these wall clocks, which, with their pretty painted scenes on the lower half were quite expensive-looking. Chauncey made them so cheaply though, that when he sent a ship-load to Britain, the customs men thought he was trying to avoid paying the proper tax by putting too low a value on his goods. They were so sure he was deceiving them that they bought the entire ship-load for Her Majesty's Government. Out of his mind with joy Chauncey immediately loaded a couple more ships with clocks in the hope that the customs men would repeat their generous offer. They did not. I wonder what happened to all those clocks?

Nineteenth century carriage clocks

Watches were probably first invented in Italy and the first wrist watch mentioned in English history was one made for Queen Elizabeth I by the royal clockmaker. But there were also small clocks made to be carried around with you, especially when travelling from one town to another, known as 'carriage' clocks. Some of the best examples are French, especially those made by the famous Leroy family of Paris, but these clocks were popular throughout Europe. By the end of the nineteenth century they were being made in steadily increasing numbers and were considered ideal gifts for weddings and retirements. The quality of these clocks is, as a rule, good, so what you buy depends on what you can afford. Prices are higher for clocks with additional mechanisms, or with a finely decorated case.

A mid-nineteenth century clock like the French one illustrated above, would cost about £450 and include a repeat button and a strike. You can tell if there is a strike mechanism or not by looking for two large brass barrels with toothed ends at or near the bottom of the works. These frequently go wrong, especially those intended to strike the quarter hours, so always check before buying by turning the hands through their full circle. If, as the minute hand passes twelve, the clock strikes an hour to which the small hour hand is not pointing, all is not lost—it can be repaired. If, on the other hand, there is nothing but silence, it is likely that some lazy devil of a repairer in the past has removed part of the strike mechanism to get the clock going again without too much trouble. By the way, look out for carriage clocks in their original leather travelling cases. This can add to their charm and value.

NOTES

invest buy shares or other things that will bring a profit
stock market building (in London) where shares in companies are bought and sold
culture the knowledge, beliefs, arts etc, that distinguish a society or nation
run in follow in one after another

reliable to be trusted
stately home the great house of an important family
carve cut shapes in wood, stone
chime make soft bell-like sounds
genuine real, not imitation
domestic from our houses

EXERCISES

Comprehension and interpretation

1 What does the writer advise people to do with their money?
2 What kinds of investment does he warn against?
3 What is the writer describing when he writes
   a a mysterious creature sits or stands in a room?
   b its young are fastened round people's wrists?
   c the creature makes a deafening noise in the early morning?
4 Explain how a human timekeeper measured the time.
5 Name some other methods of measuring time before the invention of the clock.
6 Antique clocks are a good investment. What other advantages do they have?

Use of English

Part 1 Checking the time   A day in the life of Stephen Nicholson, antique dealer.
Put the correct time next to each of the activities below and arrange in the correct order.

7 am.	went to bed
3.30 pm.	drank morning coffee
10.30 pm.	opened shop
3.15 am.	woken up by a burglar
9 am.	had tea with customer
3.30 am.	had evening meal
10.30 am.	called police
7.30 pm.	got up

Part 2 Plane arrivals
Give the am. or pm. equivalent for the following times:

8.00 hrs	13.30 hrs	20.45 hrs
23.00 hrs	2.20 hrs	17.30 hrs
1.10 hrs	13.05 hrs	11.55 hrs

Guided summary

Here are some notes about the history of clocks. Make all the changes necessary to form correct sentences which together will make a summary of the passage. Note carefully from the example what kind of alterations (if any) need to be made, especially to the words in italics.

Example 1500s watch/*make*/Queen Elizabeth 1/ royal clockmaker
Answer In the sixteenth century a watch was made for Queen Elizabeth by the royal clockmaker

Earliest ways of telling the time
human timekeeper/*measure*/time of day/heartbeat
later hours/*mark*/candles and sundials
hour glasses and water clocks/also/*use*

1600s
lantern clocks/*be*/first domestic timepieces/and these/*hang*/nail/wall
because/mechanism/often/*damage*/*protect*/ wooden case/*stand*/floor
these clocks/*pass down*/families/and/*call* grandfather clocks
first chiming mechanism/*introduce*/1696

Early 1700s
Some of best grandfather clocks/*make*/Tompion, East, Harrison
these/*make*/fine woods/and/often/beautifully/ *carve*

1800s
William Pitt/*put*/tax/domestic clocks/1797/people rely/large clocks/public places
carriage clocks/*introduce*/very useful/travelling

Vocabulary

Complete this passage with a suitable form of the word given.
It is not a good idea to leave your 1 (*save*) in the bank during a period of 2 (*inflate*). It is far better to buy 3 (*value*) antiques. Antique clocks are a very good 4 (*invest*) and it is very easy to make an interesting 5 (*collect*). Of course, you must go to a 6 (*rely*) dealer.

Discussion

How would you invest a sum of money to beat inflation?

6 The Royal Family

The way I see it

'We can't afford the Royal Family'
says WILLIE HAMILTON MP

I believe it's immoral to have a Royal family, and immoral to give them special treatment. Personally I have nothing against the Royal family—I do not dislike them as people—but some of them are paid a fortune each year and do very little to earn their £100 a day or more.

Politically the Queen now has very little power, while the Duke of Edinburgh has as much influence on important affairs of state as a country priest. It is difficult to justify paying him more than four times the salary of the Prime Minister.

Prince Charles can't spend the next twenty years just opening things, eating things or visiting things.

To justify her well-paid existence Princess Anne is always making meaningless visits.

The Queen Mother's household is second in size only to that of the Queen.

Princess Margaret makes no attempt to hide her expensive tastes and it is impossible to make out any honest case for her being much use to anybody.

The Queen is known to be among the wealthiest women in the world. It is not wealth that has been created by her own or her financial advisers' good business sense; it is wealth that has been built up by her special treatment by Parliament.

The total wealth is unknown—one of the most closely guarded secrets of modern times. No investment is ever made in the name of the Queen.

The Queen wants to keep the pretence of a Royal private household where she makes all the appointments, but she also wants the taxpayer to pay all the bills without being able to ask any questions.

—worth a fortune?

The private wealth of the Queen and her family is almost certainly more than £100 million, increasing by £10 million a year, no tax paid.

This wealth has been built up over the years because no king or queen has paid death duties since they were introduced in 1894. This is where some of the wealth comes from:
£300,000 a year from properties in the Duchy of Lancaster.

£20 million: value of the Sandringham estate (above) which covers 20,000 acres.

£150 million: value of the Crown Estate which includes shops, flats, houses, factories and mills, many in the centre of London.

£200,000 a year income for Prince Charles from the Duchy of Cornwall—but he does give the Government half.

The way we see it

'It's money well spent' says the Editor

We agree that it costs a lot of money to keep the Royal family. But the rest of Mr Hamilton's case is nonsense.

Let's look at the truth about the Queen's wealth

'Stories of a private royal fortune of £100 million or more are wildly wrong,' said the Lord Chamberlain, speaking on behalf of the Queen to a Select Committee on Royal Finance which reported to Parliament in 1971.

Mr Hamilton has forgotten inflation. Following the Committee's report, the Queen's Civil List was raised by £505,000. But since 1971 the pound has dropped in value by nearly a third. So because of inflation the £980,000 paid to the Queen under the Civil List is now worth nearer £650,000.

What the Queen pays

Pre-1971 Civil List spending was nearly £800,000. The difference was made up from the Privy Purse and the Queen's own pocket. Thanks to inflation she may yet find herself once more making a personal contribution to official expenses.

Members of the Royal family have no special protection from generally dropping values. Stock market prices have fallen sharply, so their private investments must have suffered. Property and land have dropped in value, which must include the Queen's private estates.

It is pointless to complain of the money spent on buildings like Buckingham Palace and Windsor Castle (above). The nation wants them preserved for *us*, whoever lives there. Or would Mr Hamilton tear down history?

Members of the Royal family don't do enough work? Take a look at their timetables, and add all the endless handshaking, speechmaking, travelling and homework we haven't space to record.

Moreover the Queen often spends three hours a day reading State papers and receives two deliveries of them daily wherever she is.

What do we get out of the Royal family? It's impossible to measure the value of the Royal family. Its members help the nation in ways no one else can.

Tourists bring £872 million annually into Britain. The first place they head for is Buckingham Palace (above), hoping to see the Queen.

Thousands of charities would suffer without the extensive support they receive from the Royal family.

By having the Queen as non-political Head of State, Britain is preserved from the sort of problems we see in some Republican countries. That alone is worth any sum of money Mr Hamilton cares to name.

As they take no part in politics the Royal family can, and do, act as our best Ambassadors throughout the world. This cannot be valued in pounds and pence. They express the nation's feelings. We all want to show sympathy to people injured in terrible accidents or explosions. The Royal family, by visiting the injured in hospital, do it for us.

Mr Hamilton may scorn our ancient Royal ceremonies, the sense of history, the colour and excitement the Royal family give us. But the Royal family is a basic part of the British way of life—and cheap at the price.

A year of foreign tours

THE QUEEN
Australia, New Zealand
and Indonesia.
PRINCE PHILIP
Indonesia, Switzerland,
New Zealand,
Brussels, France.
QUEEN MOTHER
Canada.
PRINCE CHARLES
Fiji, Australia.
PRINCESS ANNE
Barbados, Canada,
Australia, Germany.

Right *the Queen in the
South Sea Islands*

How the Royal family spends the taxpayers' money

(Annual costs, unless otherwise stated)

Office equipment	£46,000
Attendants at ceremonies	£71,000
Postal and phone services	£52,000
Maintenance costs of Windsor Castle	£377,584
Maintenance costs of Buckingham Palace	£385,887
The Royal train	£36,000
The Royal yacht, Britannia, since 1954	£12 million
The Royal yacht, running costs	£750,000
Princess Anne's honeymoon on the Royal yacht	£200,000
The Queen's flight, initial costs	£1,200,000
The Queen's flight, running costs	£800,000

(Prince Philip uses one of the helicopters to get
to polo matches, costing £116 an hour!)

How the Royal family earns its money

THE QUEEN 92 functions in 10 months.
Examples: Visit to Edinburgh, opened new
Police Station, visited exhibition, attended
services, visited schools.

PRINCE PHILIP 94 functions in 10 months.
Examples: Gave a lecture, went to a dinner of
the English Speaking Union, presented prizes
for design.

QUEEN MOTHER 79 functions in 11 months.
Examples: Visited schools, visited army camp,
attended Malay dinner.

PRINCESS MARGARET 71 functions in 10 months.
Examples: visited a factory, attended a charity
meeting, visited an airbase.

PRINCE CHARLES 23 functions in 11 months.
Examples: attended reception for ambassadors
in London, visited Bristol and saw ships.

PRINCESS ANNE 42 functions in 11 months.
Examples: received ambassadors at Buckingham Palace. Visited Motor Show.

NOTES

justify show that something is right
financial concerned with money
death duties taxes to be paid out of the property a dead person leaves
Lord Chamberlain the head of the royal household
on behalf of for; as representative of
Select Committee a small committee of Members of Parliament (MPs) chosen for a special inquiry
Civil List the money paid to the King or Queen for the royal household
Privy Purse the money paid to the King or Queen for private expenses

charity (an organisation handling) money given to help the poor, sick, and unfortunate
ambassador an important official representing his or her country in a foreign country
annual happening every year
maintenance keeping in a proper condition
honeymoon holiday for a newly-married man and woman
initial first
polo game played with a ball and sticks on horses
lecture speech usually made for the purpose of teaching

EXERCISES

Comprehension and discussion

From the ten statements below, list five that are for the Royal family and five that are against. Then put them in order of importance and say why you think some arguments are stronger than others.

1 The Prime Minister has a more important job than the Queen, but earns less.
2 The Queen should explain how she spends the taxpayers' money.
3 If the Royal family didn't live in their palaces, we would still want to preserve these buildings.
4 The Queen, one of the richest women in the world, ought to pay taxes.
5 The Queen spends some of her own money on official expenses.
6 Most royal visits are meaningless.
7 A non-political head of state helps national unity.
8 The Royal family waste money on their expensive tastes.
9 The Royal family attracts tourism.
10 Many charities would be poorer without the support of the Royal family.

Guided composition

Answer these questions according to the facts given in the text and combine your answers into a paragraph.

Who is the Head of State in Great Britain?
How many large estates does she own?
What are their names?
Why is Prince Philip not called King—because he does not wish to be, or because he is only the Queen's husband?
Are Prince Philip and the Duke of Edinburgh different persons or the same person?
What is the widow of the previous king called?

Does she still take an active part in public life?
What title are other male members of the Royal family given?
What about the women?
Do they take any part in public life?
Are the activities of the Royal family paid for entirely out of their own pockets, entirely by the taxpayer, or partly by both?

Use of English

Princess Anne attended 42 functions in 11 months. During that time she went on 4 royal tours, visited the Motor Show, and attended several dinners. Make two sentences like this for each of the following, matching Columns 4 and 5.

Queen	92 functions	10 months	received attended opened	several church services a new police station ambassadors at Buckingham Palace
Prince Philip	94 functions	9 months	attended presented visited	prizes at a new university five countries dinner of English Speaking Union
Queen Mother	79 functions	11 months	opened went on attended	a Malay dinner a new school a Royal tour of Canada

Vocabulary

Complete this paragraph with a suitable form of the word given in brackets.
Willie Hamilton believes it is 1 (*moral*) to give the Royal family special 2 (*treat*). He says that most of their official visits are 3 (*meaning*) and that they are far too 4 (*wealth*). The Queen's total wealth is not 5 (*know*) as no 6 (*invest*) is ever made in her name.

Discussion

Whose side are you on, Mr Hamilton's or the Editor's?

7 Energy sense makes future sense

The world is running out of oil, and energy experts believe that there could be serious shortages in ten years' time. Not only is each individual using more oil than ever before, as the standard of living in industrialised countries rises, but the population explosion means that each year many more people will be using oil in some form or other. Until recently we took oil for granted: it seemed it would never stop flowing. It was so cheap and plentiful that the whole world came to depend on it. Governments neglected other sources of energy: electricity was generated from oil and power stations were fired by it. It found its way into many of the products of light industry. Many people are surprised when they learn how many items in their homes contain oil.

The increase in the price of oil has brought the world to its senses. Governments are searching for a suitable alternative, but so far in vain. They are considering how they can make better use of the two other major fuels, coal and natural gas, but they have found that neither can take the place of oil in their economies. In recent years there has been a growing concern for the environment and coal is not a popular fuel with environmentalists. Coal mines are ugly, and their development has a serious effect on animal and plant life; coal itself is a heavy pollutant. Natural gas, the purest of the three fuels, is also the most limited in supply.

The answer would seem to lie in nuclear power stations. They need very little fuel to produce enormous amounts of power and they do not pollute the atmosphere. Their dangers, however, are so great and the cost of building them so high that some governments are unwilling to invest in them. Not only could one accident in a single nuclear power station spread as much radio-activity as a thousand Hiroshima atom bombs, but the radio-active waste from these stations is extremely dangerous—for one hundred thousand years. So is there no possible alternative to nuclear power?

Well, there are several, but none of them seems likely to satisfy future world energy demands. Scientists have recently turned their attention to natural sources of energy: the sun, the sea, the wind and hot springs. Of these the sun seems the most promising source for the future. Houses have already been built which are heated entirely by solar energy. However, solar energy can only be collected during daylight hours, and in countries where the weather is unreliable, an alternative heating system has to be included.

Experiments are being carried out at the University of Arizona on ways of storing solar energy on a large scale. To satisfy a large part of the energy needs of a country like America, huge power stations covering 5,000 square miles would have to be built and one wonders whether this would be acceptable to environmentalists. While experiments in generating energy from the sea and the wind are interesting, neither can be considered an obvious solution to a future energy crisis; the first because a lot of energy is needed to generate energy from the sea, and the second because the amount of energy generated from wind would satisfy only a small percentage of a nation's needs.

Another source of energy which could be more widely used is that generated by hot water or steam from under the earth (geothermal energy as it is called). This form of energy is already being used in New Zealand, Iceland, the Soviet Union and very successfully in Italy, where it generates a quarter of the nation's electricity.

Many scientists are optimistic that new ways of generating large amounts of energy will be successfully developed, but at the same time they fear the consequences. If the world population goes on increasing at its present rate, and each individual continues to use more energy every year, we may, in fifty years' time, be burning up so much energy that we would damage the earth's atmosphere. By raising the temperature of the atmosphere, we could melt the Arctic and Antarctic ice-caps and change the pattern of vegetable and animal life throughout the world— a frightening possibility.

How to stop your car over-eating.

These days, we just can't afford to let our cars guzzle more fuel than they should. Use these simple suggestions to help you Save It–save energy.

Use minimum choke. And shut it off as soon as you can. We can't afford to burn up petrol at today's prices.

Regular servicing costs money. But it'll keep your car running at peak efficiency, which will pay you in the long run.

Don't race away from the lights. It wastes fuel. And you'll only be first at the next red light!

If you can, avoid rush hours. Sitting in traffic jams uses petrol and doesn't get you anywhere.

Sharing a car with work mates can save a small fortune in fuel. (It means fewer cars on the road too.) Take it in turns to provide the transport.

It really does pay to keep to the new speed limits. A car travelling at 50mph can use 30% less petrol than at 70mph.

If you can, leave your car at home for short trips. It'll slim your fuel bills. And you too!

Don't forget to Save It at work too. Not just in motoring, but anywhere you see energy being wasted.

Steady driving saves fuel. Anticipate hazards and avoid harsh braking.

Energy sense is common sense.

Issued by the Department of Energy.

These dangers will have to be kept in mind as scientists continue with their experiments. In the meantime, we can all help to protect the environment by not wasting energy. This means driving more carefully (if you *have* to use a car—it's healthier and cheaper to ride a bike) and turning off unnecessary lighting and heating in the home. In these small ways we can all help to make the world a cleaner, healthier place for future generations.

The man who tried

Bill Sandey, a builder, has a plan for cutting the cost of living. He wants to put up an 'independent' house, which would supply the people living in it with free heat, gas, electricity, water and food.

Mr Sandey, aged 53, plans just a one-bedroom house, for himself and his wife, but even on that scale he says he could grow nearly 1,000 kilos of vegetables and fruit a year.

The town council, however, has refused him permission to build the house where he wants, in the back garden of his present home. Two houses in one garden is disapproved of, he has been told, and a three-storey building might upset the neighbours.

'Red tape' says Mr Sandey. 'When will officials learn that this sort of thing is the only way ahead for a wasteful world running out of energy?'

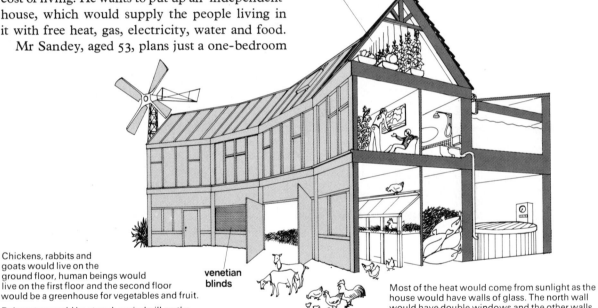

greenhouse

venetian blinds

Chickens, rabbits and goats would live on the ground floor, human beings would live on the first floor and the second floor would be a greenhouse for vegetables and fruit.

Rainwater would be stored, a windmill on the roof would provide electricity, and the waste would go through a special machine to produce methane gas for cooking and heating, and fertilizer for the plants.

Most of the heat would come from sunlight as the house would have walls of glass. The north wall would have double windows and the other walls would have special venetian blinds, either letting the sun's rays through or keeping the warmth in. This would produce near-tropical conditions in the greenhouse.

NOTES

run out of come to the end of
take for granted accept without question
generate produce
item thing (as part of a list)
major big; of great importance
nuclear power station a place where electricity is produced by division of atoms
radio-active sending out dangerous rays
obvious quite clear

percentage the number in each hundred (%)
crisis time of danger
optimistic expecting the best
consequence result
guzzle eat or drink quickly and noisily
in the long run in the end
generation all the people born about the same time
fertilizer a preparation of substances to make soil richer
red tape silly rules that delay business

EXERCISES

Comprehension

Choose the best answer in the following

1 The world *a* has run out of oil; *b* did run out of oil; *c* will never run out of oil; *d* is running out of oil.
2 The main disadvantage of coal is that *a* it is not expensive; *b* there is not enough of it; *c* it is a heavy pollutant; *d* it is too easy to mine.
3 Natural gas cannot replace oil because *a* supplies are limited; *b* it is a heavy pollutant; *c* it is very expensive; *d* it is dangerous to use.
4 Nuclear power stations *a* pollute the atmosphere; *b* often explode; *c* produce extremely dangerous waste; *d* are inexpensive to build.
5 We should save energy by *a* driving faster; *b* not stopping at traffic lights; *c* having our cars regularly serviced; *d* driving slowly in traffic jams.

Use of English

Part 1 . . . not only . . . but . . .
Join a sentence from Column B to one from Column A. The sentences must support the same argument.
Note the position of *not only* after the verb *to be*:
Example Riding a bike is cheap. It saves petrol.
Answer Riding a bike is not only cheap, but it saves petrol.
but *before* other verbs: Riding a bike not only makes you tired, but is dangerous.

Column A	*Column B*
Oil is our main source of energy	Coal mines are ugly
Coal is a heavy pollutant	Many items in the home contain it
Riding a bike saves money	It wastes petrol
Natural gas is cheaper than oil	It will save you a fortune
Fast driving causes accidents	It is the cleanest of the three fuels
Sharing a car with friends is fun	It keeps you healthy

Part 2 Not only . . . but
Now do the sentences again beginning with *Not only* . . . followed by a verb.
Answer Not only is coal expensive, but it pollutes the atmosphere
Not only does it cost a lot, but supplies are limited

Guided summary

Fill in the blanks in the following dialogue in which Bill Sandey is being interviewed by a journalist:
What will be on the ground floor?
That's where the animals will live. I'll keep ____ ____ and ____ .
Will you keep them as pets or for economic reasons?
For economic reasons. I'll get ____ from the chickens, I'll ____ the rabbits and ____ the goats
You say your wife and yourself will live on the first floor, but what about your second floor?
That will be a ____ . I expect to ____ 1,000 kilos of ____ and ____ each year.
You say the walls will be made of glass, but how will you keep warm?
Heat will come ____ ____ . The north wall will have ____ ____ and the other walls will have ____ venetian ____ .
Where will you get water and electricity from?
Rainwater ____ ____ ____ and a windmill ____ ____ ____ .
What will you do with your waste?
It will go ____ ____ special machine ____ ____ methane gas. This will be used ____ ____ and ____ .
It all sounds fine, What is preventing you from building this house?
____ ____ !

Discussion

Can you think of other ways we can save energy?

8 Food for thought

William Green looks at the world food crisis with the help of Dr Tom Scott, an agricultural expert who has been working in India, Professor Brian Hawkes, a crop scientist from Leeds University, and Clare Knight, a home economist from 'Housewife' magazine.

GREEN Millions of people have starved to death in recent years. Many more live miserable lives because they don't get enough food, or food of the right kind. If we can't feed all the people alive in the world today, what's going to happen as a result of the population explosion?

SCOTT I don't think we should be too pessimistic about the future. World food production is increasing every year.

HAWKES That's true, but it's not increasing as fast as the world population. This graph shows this only too clearly. What's more, the extra food being produced is going to people who don't need it—overweight British schoolchildren, for example.

TOTAL AND PER CAPITA FOOD PRODUCTION 1961–72

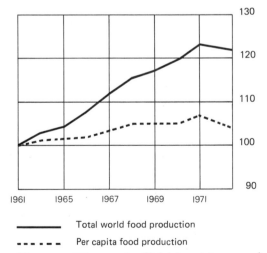

——— Total world food production

- - - - - Per capita food production

SCOTT Yes, we all know the British eat too much sugar and chocolate. But I'm concerned with foods like rice. Rice is the staple food of 60% of the world's population and really exciting work is going on in developing new varieties of this cereal. Agriculturalists are really pleased with the results we're getting from the new high-yield types of rice.

HAWKES Mm. But don't forget that the seeds of these new high-yield cereals like wheat and rice are more expensive, so poor farmers can't afford to buy them. Not to mention the fact that without the right amount of water at the right time of year the harvest may be worse than with traditional varieties.

SCOTT But governments are making great progress with irrigation schemes in many parts of the world. These difficulties *can* be overcome.

HAWKES That's only half the story. These high-yield cereals need a lot of good fertilizer too, and people...

SCOTT Yes, I know, but nowadays we don't have any difficulty in persuading people to use modern fertilizers and pesticides.

HAWKES I'm sure you don't. They just can't afford to buy them, that's all. Prices have shot up recently. The cost of raw materials used in fertilizers and pesticides has increased, to say nothing of manufacturing and transport costs.

SCOTT Well, several developing countries have found a way of dealing with the last two points you mention. They are setting up their own small · factories to produce fertilizers and pesticides locally.

GREEN Shall we turn to another hopeful development? Food technologists have now found ways of making soya beans look, feel and taste like meat.

SCOTT That's right. These beans have a much higher protein content than cereal crops, and if we could persuade people in developing countries to change their diet and eat soya beans, we could make them a lot healthier.

HAWKES It's an expensive process making soya beans tasty, and plenty of people don't like

Right *tasty TVP pies*, below *high yield wheat in the Andes*

them even then. In fact, it's extremely difficult to persuade people to change their eating habits. After all, would *you* give up eating steak for the rest of your life?

SCOTT No, but I *have* already decided to eat less meat. As you know, it takes nearly 4 kilos of vegetable or grain protein to produce half a kilo of meat protein. Indeed, it's been calculated that if everyone in Europe, America, Russia and Japan ate one hamburger less a week there'd be enough grain to relieve all the starving people in India and Bangladesh.

HAWKES Well, the students at my university have demanded one meatless meal a week, but unfortunately the world doesn't consist of idealistic students. How do we get the grain that's saved to the places where it's needed? Transport costs have risen astronomically since oil prices went up. Who's going to pay to send food round the world? I must say I find your views unbelievably optimistic.

GREEN Well, optimist or pessimist, I'm sure we all agree that this is a world problem and needs a world solution. Governments must get together and work out ways of dealing with the food crisis, and there are already signs of increasing international effort here. Nationally, we're making progress here in Britain. There's

a growing use of soya bean 'meat' in hospital and school meals. A restaurant opened in London recently serving only meatless meals. Perhaps you'd like to say a bit more about this development, Clare?

CLARE KNIGHT Yes, well, we're all eating more soya beans than we realise already. You've probably seen pictures like this before, but there's a big difference in this photo [above] —the basic ingredient in all these attractive dishes is man-made. Modern industrial techniques, similar to those used in the manufacture of man-made fibres like nylon, turn vegetable protein into a substance, Textured Vegetable Protein, or TVP for short, that looks, feels and tastes like meat.

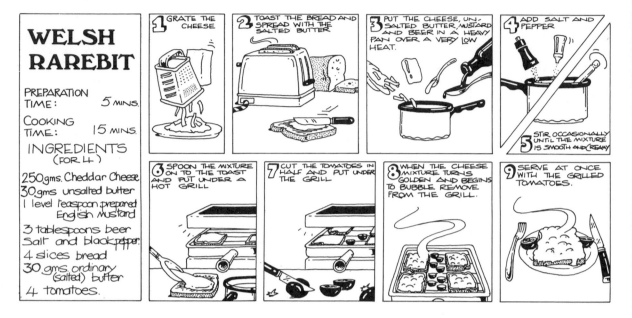

WELSH RAREBIT

PREPARATION TIME: 5 MINS.

COOKING TIME: 15 MINS.

INGREDIENTS (FOR 4)

250 gms. Cheddar Cheese
30 gms unsalted butter
1 level teaspoon prepared English mustard
3 tablespoons beer
Salt and black pepper
4 slices bread
30 gms. ordinary (salted) butter
4 tomatoes.

1 GRATE THE CHEESE

2 TOAST THE BREAD AND SPREAD WITH THE SALTED BUTTER

3 PUT THE CHEESE, UNSALTED BUTTER, MUSTARD AND BEER IN A HEAVY PAN OVER A VERY LOW HEAT.

4 ADD SALT AND PEPPER

5 STIR OCCASIONALLY UNTIL THE MIXTURE IS SMOOTH AND CREAMY

6 SPOON THE MIXTURE ON TO THE TOAST AND PUT UNDER A HOT GRILL

7 CUT THE TOMATOES IN HALF AND PUT UNDER THE GRILL

8 WHEN THE CHEESE MIXTURE TURNS GOLDEN AND BEGINS TO BUBBLE REMOVE FROM THE GRILL.

9 SERVE AT ONCE WITH THE GRILLED TOMATOES.

GREEN Really? You mean I could be eating chicken pie, but it wouldn't be chicken pie at all, but TVP pie?

CLARE KNIGHT That's it. TVP is sold in various flavours, beef, pork, or chicken, is cheaper than meat and easier to prepare—you simply heat it up.

GREEN Can you buy it in the shops?

CLARE KNIGHT Not very easily yet, not for the ordinary housewife, but women who care about the food crisis can easily serve their family meatless meals—this traditional recipe [see above] for Welsh rarebit is a great favourite with my family.

GREEN Thank you, Clare. I'll make that for my wife and myself this weekend. I certainly agree that eating meatless meals is one way individuals can help the world food crisis, but it won't solve the world food problem. Neither will growing new sorts of rice. Next time I'll be looking at some of the long-term possibilities for producing more food. Scientists may be able to find ways of controlling the weather; then we'll be able to save our harvests from droughts or floods. We may even be able to make the African deserts green or melt the Arctic ice and grow food there. Then there's the sea. Man has eaten fish for centuries, but there's a wealth of other food waiting beneath the oceans. Finally, it has even been suggested that we may be able to live on other planets, a suggestion that certainly gives us food for thought!

NOTES

starve die from lack of food
home economist one who has studied the science of getting the best value and the best results in keeping a home, feeding a family, etc.
pessimistic expecting the worst
per capita for each person
staple main food for supporting human life
traditional handed down from generation to generation

irrigation scheme a (proposed) way of bringing water to the land by canals or other artificial means
pesticide substance that kills harmful insects etc.
protein substances present in such foods as meat and eggs, that help to keep the body healthy
astronomically immensely (as in *astronomy*, the study of the stars and the immense distances of space)
ingredient substance used in cooking

EXERCISES

Comprehension

Which of these statements are true and which false?

1 Millions of people have starved to death in recent years
2 Food production is increasing faster than world population
3 British schoolchildren are overweight because they eat too much rice
4 The staple diet of 60% of the world's population is rice
5 Most poor farmers are growing the new high yield types of rice
6 Food technologists have found ways of making meat taste like soya beans
7 If people in developing countries ate one hamburger less a week there would be no food crisis
8 In Britain soya bean meat is being eaten in hospitals and schools

Use of English

Clare Knight in the kitchen talking about things that can easily happen and probably will.
Example If you are interested in meatless meals...
Answer If you *are interested* in meatless meals, you *will like* this.
Complete the following.

1 If housewives regularly serve meatless meals, they ___ money
2 If you are a vegetarian, you ___ this Welsh rarebit
3 Your family will want to try this recipe, if ___ English food
4 The Welsh rarebit will be tastier, if you ___ some mustard
5 If you ___ occasionally, the mixture ___ smooth and creamy
6 It will not taste good, if you ___ the salt and pepper
7 The cheese on top will burn, if you ___ the Welsh rarebit under the grill too long
8 It will make a delicious meal, if you ___ it with grilled tomatoes

The pessimist's view: things that could happen, but probably will not.
Example If Dr Scott were right, there...
Answer If Dr Scott *were* right there *would be* no problem.

1 If all the people in developed countries ate less meat...
2 If the price of fertilisers fell, ...
3 If British schoolchildren did not eat so many chocolates...
4 If we could make African deserts green...
5 If scientists could control the weather...
6 If we could persuade people in developing countries to eat soya beans...
7 There would be enough food, if the population ...
8 Developing countries would use modern fertilisers, if...

Guided summary

Complete these two letters written to a newspaper that had printed an article on food production.

Dear Sir,
The writer of your article on world food production does not seem to know much about the progress being made in this field. Here are some reasons why I am more optimistic than he is. Food production ___ every year. Agriculturalists ___ new high-yield types of rice and many governments ___ their irrigation schemes. Many countries are now not only ___ modern fertilisers and pesticides, but they ___ them themselves. Food technologists ___ ways of making soya beans taste like meat. One further hopeful development is that many young people in developed countries ___ to eat less meat so that there will be more grain for the starving.
Yours optimistically,
Dr T. Scott

Dear Sir,
I am afraid I disagree with Dr Tom Scott. Food production is not ___ as fast as ___ . The new high-yield types of rice are both ___ and also need ___ . They must also have a lot of good fertiliser and ___ . While it is true that food technologists ___ , it is very difficult ___ . I cannot deny that many idealistic people, both young and old, ___ , but Dr Scott has forgotten ___ .
Yours pessimistically,
Prof. B. Hawkes

Discussion

Do you really think there is a world food crisis? Give reasons for your answer.

THE TRAMP
AND THE
PHILOSOPHER

THE GOLDRUSH 1925

The idea for one of the funniest scenes in this film came from a true story. A group of men heading for California to find gold, got lost in the snow in the Sierra Nevada mountains and ate their shoes when they were starving. In the film Charlie boils his shoe as if it was a tasty chicken, picks at the nails as if they were bones and eats the shoelaces as though they were spaghetti.

THE CIRCUS 1928

In this film Charlie performs some very amusing and clever tricks. Here we see him performing dangerous stunts on a high wire, when he has to appear instead of the star acrobat at a circus. He is not helped by the monkeys pulling his hair and standing on his hands. Later he is caught in a cage and has to try to escape — the only problem is that there is a sleeping lion in his way.

In 1911 a penniless young music-hall artist left England for America. His future was uncertain, but he did not believe it could be unhappier than his past. He had grown up in the slums of London's East End and experienced great poverty. His mother's life had been so hard that she had finally gone mad, and his father had died of drink. Both parents had been on the stage and lived in the hope that they would one day be 'stars'. Their son was determined to succeed where they had failed.

By 1914 his optimism and determination were justified. Charles Chaplin was the most talked-about man in America, the king of silent movies. He was not only admired as a first-class actor and comedian, he was also making his name as a director. How did he reach the top of the film world in such a short time? He was not an instant success. His attempts to copy other slapstick comedians who were popular at that time were a failure. However he gradually began to develop the character of the tramp that we always connect with his name. He borrowed ideas from many sources and though he 'stole' most of his clothes from other slapstick come-dians of the time, he developed his own special mannerisms to go with them. He used his bowler hat to signal secret messages and his walking stick allowed him to cause confusion and punish his enemy from a distance. He got the idea for his famous flat-footed walk from a London taxi driver who had sore feet.

Charlie, the tramp, looked very funny, but he was also lovable. Inside his tramp's clothes, the audience saw a human being who was poor but dreamt of being rich, who was ugly but wanted to be handsome, who was lonely and desperately wanted a girlfriend. The tramp was a great romantic, but he always lost his heart to girls who for some reason had to leave him. The audience would be moved by this, but before they had time to reach for their handkerchiefs, Charlie's feet would get in the way and they would laugh instead.

In his early days as a director, Chaplin pro-duced sixty-two short silent comedy films in four years. He had complete control of his work and he could use his many gifts as he wished. He was a master of the art of mime and as an acrobat used to perform many dangerous stunts.

43

The first film in which the audience hear the tramp's voice when he sings a nonsense song. Charlie is at his most amusing when we see him working harder and harder and faster and faster to keep up with the machine. The film criticises the cruelty of factory life.

But his greatest gift was his sense of timing—something which he said had come to him from his mother, who had been a dancer.

In 1919 he formed his own film company, which means that he owned every film he made. He began to take much longer to make his films. If an idea did not come, or a detail was wrong, he would send everybody home until he had found a solution. His films began to be more serious. He wanted to write about his own experiences and show how unjust life was.

In *The Kid*, which is about an orphan, Chaplin remembered his own fear and unhappiness when he was separated from his mother. Then, in 1929, the Wall Street Stock Market collapsed. Suddenly there were tramps like Charlie everywhere, and the cruel division between rich and poor is reflected in the opening scene of *City Lights*. Chaplin now felt the need to comment on the fate of the world as well as on the life of his hero. At this time he made *The Great Dictator* which made fun of Hitler's philosophy and mannerisms. He described Hitler as 'this amazing imitation of me'. Extreme right-wing people in America persuaded the American people through the press that Chaplin was too left-wing. His next film, *Monsieur Verdoux* was not popular, and

Chaplin said: 'I felt I had. . .the hate of a whole nation and that my film career was lost.'

When he was on a visit to Britain the American government refused to give him a re-entry visa. So in 1948 he decided to make his home in Switzerland. His marriage to the lovely Oona O'Neill was happy, and he became the proud father of eight children. Nevertheless he still felt bitter and the films he continued to make show this. *The King in New York* is the story of a king living in a foreign country who is made to suffer for his beliefs. America still suspected Chaplin's political beliefs and his films were not shown there. But Chaplin denied having a political philosophy: 'I have no design for living, no philosophy. Whether wise or foolish, we must all struggle with life.'

It was not until 1972 that Chaplin and Hollywood finally made up their quarrel and he was invited back to receive an apology—and the award of an Oscar. He was given a hero's welcome and was deeply moved by it. Then, in 1975, aged 86, he returned to London, the city of his birth. He went to Buckingham Palace to be knighted by the Queen. Charlie, the tramp, would have fallen over as he left. Sir Charles Chaplin simply wept.

NOTES

tramp a person without work or home who walks from one place to another
music hall theatre for mixed entertainment (popular song, dance, humour etc.)
slapstick funny acting with a lot of fast, noisy actions
mannerism peculiar tricks of behaviour
mime acting without words
acrobat a person skilled in walking on ropes or swinging between ropes high in the air, balancing, walking on hands, etc, as an entertainment

stunt a daring and dangerous action (especially in the cinema)
orphan child without one or (usually) both parents
Wall Street Stock Market The New York centre for buying and selling shares
collapse fall down suddenly
comment explain or speak about a subject
career what one works at in life
visa a form giving permission to enter or leave a country
award (**n**) prize (**v**) to give a prize
Oscar American prize for the best film, film actor, etc., of the year

EXERCISES

Comprehension

Which of these statements are true and which false?
1 Chaplin was born in America _F – last pan,_
2 He grew up in London's West End _F – East,_
3 His parents were rich _F – T_
4 His slapstick comedy was immediately successful _F – 2 failure_
5 He directed a lot of films _T – 4_
6 His films were not popular in America in the mid forties _T 6_
7 He made his home in Switzerland in 1948 _T – 7_
8 The British knighted him _T – 8_

Use of English verb + object + —ing

In this film we see Charlie dancing.
Rewrite these sentences beginning with the words in brackets and using this pattern.
1 In 'The Circus' Charlie performs some clever tricks, tries to escape from a lion's cage, and walks nervously across a high wire. (In this film we see . . .)
2 In 'Modern Times' Charlie sings a nonsense song and is fed by a machine. (In this we hear . . . and we watch . . .)
3 In 'The Great Dictator' Charlie makes fun of Hitler's philosophy and imitates his mannerisms. (In this film the audience sees . . .)
4 In 'Goldrush' Charlie looks for gold, gets lost in the snow and eats his shoe. (This film shows . . .)
5 In 'The King in New York' a king has to live in a foreign country and suffers for his beliefs. (In this film Chaplin describes . . .)

Complete the following passage with suitable prepositions
When he was 22 Chaplin left England 1 __ America. He soon became admired 2 __ an actor, comedian and director. In his early work as a director he worked very fast producing 62 films 3 __ four years. However it is the figure of the tramp that we always connect 4 __ his name. The tramp is both lovable and amusing: his feet always get 5 __ the way, his cane punishes his enemy 6 __ a distance. In some of his films Chaplin comments 7 __ the fate of the world and in others he tells 8 __ his own experiences.

Vocabulary

Complete the following passage by putting the words in brackets into a suitable form.

Charlie was not an instant 1 (*succeed*) in Hollywood. His early attempts to copy other comedians were a 2 (*fail*). He became famous as the tramp and made many 3 (*amuse*) films in this part. His more serious films are concerned with the cruel 4 (*divide*) between rich and poor. After the war the American government refused to give him a re-entry visa because some people thought his 5 (*politics*) views were too left wing. In 1972 he received a public 6 (*apologise*) from Hollywood in the form of a special Oscar.

Discussion

Discuss the life and work of other famous film stars.

EARTHQUAKE SHATTERS AGADIR

Thousands were killed and injured when a violent earthquake shattered the Moroccan port of Agadir last night, the Moroccan Navy reported in Rabat today. A Navy message from the ruined town said that 90% of the buildings in the suburbs and about 70% of those in the modern quarter, known as the 'New Town' have been destroyed. The number of casualties is extremely high.

Hundreds of injured have been taken to Agadir airport where an emergency medical centre has been set up. Many people are still trapped in the ruins. The situation is particularly serious since the police and army, who would normally help in the emergency, have suffered heavy losses themselves. The city's fire engines have been destroyed and the harbour is out of action. Telephone communications have been wrecked as well.

A pilot who flew over the area reported, 'The city looks as if a giant foot has stepped on it and crushed it flat.'

Another report from the city said that two out of every three buildings in the European quarter have been destroyed and all buildings higher than three storeys have been damaged.

A hospital in Casablanca has prepared three hundred beds for some of the casualties who will be flown there today.

BURIED ALIVE

March 4 Casablanca I was present last night when a young woman, who had been trapped under more than ten metres of broken concrete for two days, was brought to the surface. 23 year-old Sue Evans was on holiday with her husband and baby daughter when the earthquake struck. They had just unpacked their suitcases on the top floor of the Hotel Saada and while Sue was in the bathroom combing her hair, her husband was talking to the baby in the bedroom. It was 11.40 pm.

As Sue was looking at herself in the mirror, she heard a terrible roar that sounded like an enormous underground train rushing through the hotel. The mirror shattered and huge cracks appeared in the walls. As she tried to reach her husband she found herself being pressed down under a heavy weight.

After some time the noise stopped, and in the darkness and the silence Sue realised with horror that she had been buried alive under several tons of concrete. In the hours that followed she could see no hope for herself and she had no idea whether her husband and child were still alive.

Some twenty-four hours later, after several desperate attempts, a young Frenchman finally reached her. He had risked his life by digging a way through the ruins. By this time Sue was in a deep state of shock and close to death.

The rescuers realised that it would take several hours to free her. The young Frenchman had to keep her awake somehow. He kept her alive by telling her about Paris and promising to give her and her family a wonderful time there when she got out. He kept telling her that her husband and child were safe.

At last the moment came when she was pulled free and pushed upwards from one pair of helping hands to another. Sue explained later, 'I thought I was being pushed up into heaven.'

What can we learn from Agadir?

Following our story about the Agadir earthquake, we have had many letters on the subject. Here are answers to some of your questions.

Your account of the earthquake at Agadir made me wonder if scientists know where an earthquake will take place, and whether they know how destructive it will be. I have heard that minor tremors usually occur before a major earthquake. If this is true, why wasn't it possible to warn the people of Agadir before the earthquake struck?

Scientists use special instruments, seismographs, to measure movement under the ground. When an earthquake occurs, shock waves travel round the earth and scientists record these according to an international scale of intensity: (1939 Turkey 7.9; 1960 Chile 8.9 etc.) The shock at Agadir was too small to show on a seismograph in time to warn the people of Agadir. However, the earthquake occurred very close to the surface and Agadir was directly above it. It was therefore very destructive, or as scientists would say, very 'intense'. The international scale of intensities is shown on the next page.

I am puzzled that buildings in both the local and the European style collapsed so easily at Agadir, when so much progress has been made in designing buildings for earthquake areas. Was the force of the earthquake too strong for these designs or had they not been used?

Experience has shown that certain types of building resist earthquakes better than others. They should either be very solid (reinforced concrete) or 'elastic' (wood or woven branches). It is quite true that earthquake-proof buildings have been designed and we have seen in Chile, Japan and California, and in other places, that these resist earthquakes much better than normal buildings. Most people in Agadir lived in houses with earth walls. The roofs were supported by heavy beams which killed many as they fell. The European-style buildings had not been designed for an earthquake area.

I was deeply moved to read of the experience of Sue Evans who was on holiday with her husband at Agadir when the earthquake struck. Although we have had no experience of serious earthquakes in England, many of us spend our holidays in Portugal, Turkey and North Africa where major earthquakes have occurred. Where else do major earthquakes sometimes occur? I would also like to know what one should do if one is in a town that is struck.

Of all recorded earthquakes 90% have occurred in one of two areas, a belt surrounding the Pacific Ocean and another stretching from the Alps to the Himalayas.

It is difficult to give people advice on what to do in an earthquake. If you have time it is best to head for the open countryside. If the tremor is sudden and severe your best hope is to get under a heavy table or bed. Doorways and windows collapse first and people hurrying out of a house may be hit by these.

The international scale of intensities

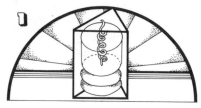

A shock recorded by seismographs only: unnoticed by man.

A shock felt by a few people here and there, particularly those on the higher floors of buildings.

A shock strong enough for its length and direction to be measured.

A shock noticed by many people indoors: cups and saucers rattle, floors and ceilings crack.

A shock noticed by everyone; furniture shakes, some bells ring.

People asleep are woken up and run out of their houses in alarm. Lights swing, clocks stop, trees shake, plaster falls.

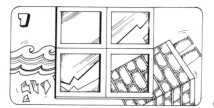

Weak chimneys fall; window-panes break; waves appear in smooth water; houses made of wood and woven branches are undamaged.

Statues turn round; church towers and factory chimneys fall; rocks fall from heights.

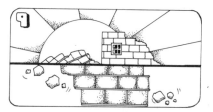

Total destruction of a few buildings. European-style buildings are seriously damaged; some can no longer be lived in.

Most stone buildings are destroyed; bridges are damaged; main water and gas pipes are broken; deep holes appear in streets; landslides on slopes and banks.

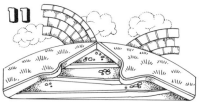

Stone buildings are completely destroyed; a few wood and branch buildings remain standing. All bridges fall; railway lines are twisted.

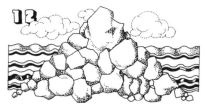

Nothing is left of man-made things; huge falls of rock; lakes are formed.

NOTES

shatter destroy violently
suburbs outlying part of a city
casualties people who have been killed, wounded or made ill
emergency sudden happening which makes it necessary to act without delay
storey floor of a building

minor small; of less importance
tremor shake
seismograph machine to measure earth tremors
occur happen
rattle make the noise of something hard shaken against another hard object
statue stone or metal figure of a person

EXERCISES

Comprehension

Which of the following statements are true and which false?

1 Scientists have to be very near an earthquake to measure it
2 An earthquake's effect depends on the depth of the tremor, the distance from the town and the strength of the buildings
3 Many lives would not have been lost in Agadir if the buildings had been stronger
4 There are no areas which have more earthquakes than others
5 When an earthquake strikes it is advisable to get into bed
6 If your house is struck by an earthquake you should stand in the doorway
7 People on higher floors notice tremors more quickly than people on lower floors
8 Minor tremors are more noticeable indoors than outdoors

Guided composition

Imagine you are a science correspondent answering listeners' questions on a phone-in radio programme. Give short simple answers to the following questions.

1 Agadir was shattered by a minor tremor. Why was a small tremor so destructive?
2 In which parts of the world have most earthquakes occurred?
3 What should I do if my house is suddenly struck by an earthquake?
4 I live in an earthquake area. What sort of house should I build?
5 What factors influence the intensity of an earthquake?
6 How do scientists many miles from an earth tremor know that one is taking place?

Use of English

Complete the following by filling each blank with a verb in a suitable form. Do not use any verb more than once.

Radio correspondent: I have just visited the scene of the earthquake. I am sad to report that hundreds of people ____ or ____ . Many ____ as they lay in their beds. Many houses ____ completely ____ when the first tremor struck. Fortunately the main hospital ____ , but it is already full. Many casualties ____ to an emergency medical centre at the airport. The most serious casualties ____ from the airport to Casablanca. Rescue operations have been difficult because telephone communications ____ and main gas and water pipes ____ . Rescuers fear that many people ____ still ____ in the ruins.

Vocabulary

Complete the following with suitable forms of the words in brackets. Sue felt herself being pressed down under a heavy 1 (*weigh*). Soon the noise ended and in the 2 (*dark*) and 3 (*silent*) she realised she had been buried 4 (*live*). Rescuers made several 5 (*despair*) attempts to reach her and were finally 6 (*succeed*).

Discussion

Have you ever faced an emergency?
What other emergencies should people be prepared for?

WASTE NOT WANT NOT

Is this the best we can do with our rubbish?

We are offering readers the opportunity to give their views on any subject they feel strongly about. This week's contributor is Mrs Jane Holt, housewife and mother

Can you believe it? There's a world paper shortage, there's a national bottle shortage, and we're running out of raw materials like timber and tin—or so the papers say. Well, I've just emptied my shopping basket after my weekly shopping trip and it was full of things made from these scarce materials. Half of what I'd bought I threw away at once: all those unnecessary paper bags, plastic bags, fresh wrapping paper and old newspapers they put the food in nowadays.

You can't even buy a loaf of bread without getting a piece of paper round it—that's if you can find a loaf that hasn't already been sliced and then wrapped. Supermarkets are the worst offenders. Pieces of meat are put on small plastic trays and then wrapped in polythene, cartons of cream are put in extra paper bags at the check-out point, fruit and vegetables are packed in plastic bags, cheese is sold wrapped in polythene and eggs come in special cardboard or plastic boxes. Some things are double-packed by the manufacturer: tins of fish come in small cardboard boxes, breakfast cereals are packed in plastic bags inside cardboard containers.

All this packaging makes shopping cleaner and more convenient, but at what cost? Every time you throw away a paper bag you're throwing away part of a tree—and trees don't grow overnight! At this rate there soon won't be any trees left, and then what shall we do?

Perhaps we'll learn to do what my mother did.

She used to keep a store of paper bags in a kitchen drawer and use them again and again for her shopping. Most goods were sold loose in those days and the shopkeeper weighed out the amount you wanted.

Why can't manufacturers today cut down on the amount of packaging they use? I know they *say* their goods are double—and even triple—wrapped because their customers prefer this, but have they actually asked the customers what they think? Someone must pay for all that packaging and I suspect it's you and me. Given the choice the average housewife would rather get food than plastic bags for her money.

Of course, liquid goods have always been sold in bottles, jars or cans, but why can't we use these containers more than once? There have been attempts to replace the familiar British milk bottle with cartons, but in most parts of the country the milkman still delivers our milk in bottles and collects the empties the next day. Why don't we re-use our wine and beer bottles too?

In fact, when I was a little girl I used to get extra pocket-money by returning bottles to the shops for a penny each. If we re-used all our bottles we would save on the raw materials and energy needed to make new ones. Surely shops and supermarkets could organise the collection of empty bottles and jam-jars for return to the manufacturers? If they can't, or won't, why don't local councils improve the system of rubbish collection? We could sort out all the things that could be used again—bottles and jars, and make special piles of clean paper and old cans that can be recycled.

If that's too complicated, then the government should consider other ways of salvaging raw materials from our rubbish, or at least putting it to better use. At the moment 90% of our rubbish is just dumped, sometimes near well-known beauty spots. In Japan they crush their rubbish, coat it in concrete and use it for making roads. In Sweden whole blocks of flats are heated by burning domestic rubbish in special incinerators, and in America they've found a way of obtaining oil and gas from rubbish. They don't waste their waste but are finding new fuels. It's time we started to think seriously about the growing shortage of raw materials in the world today and stopped this mad destruction of our environment by our throw-away society.

We have invited three people to comment on Mrs Holt's views

A Government spokesman

On behalf of my department I should like to say how pleased we are when members of the public take an interest in matters of the environment. Mrs Holt is, of course, quite right to be concerned about the waste of raw materials caused by modern packaging but I regret to say that the solutions she suggests all cost money—taxpayers' money. In fact, my department is considering three main ways of improving this situation, but so far they have all proved very expensive.

Firstly we could re-use all our bottles, as Mrs Holt suggests, but it would cost a lot of money to sort them according to shape and size

and we do not feel we can spare the money for this at present. It would be considerably easier if bottles were produced in standard sizes, as they are in Germany and elsewhere, and we are encouraging manufacturers to consider this.

Secondly, we could make greater efforts to collect scrap tin and waste paper for recycling. Several local councils are experimenting with new ways of collecting domestic rubbish, but it's proving very costly.

Thirdly, we could burn our rubbish in special incinerators and extract various substances from it. Again, some local councils have already bought special machinery to sort out metal and glass waste from the rubbish collections. The Americans and Scandinavians are ahead of us in this, but their experiments, though interesting and encouraging, are proving very expensive. My department is watching all these current experiments with great interest, and Mrs Holt can be sure that we will certainly consider any ideas that make financial sense.

A representative from a food manufacturer

Well, of course, the basic problem is cost. It's all very well for Mrs Holt to say that the average housewife would prefer her money to go on the contents of the package rather then the packaging. My company has done quite a lot of market research on this question, and results have shown that goods that are generously and attractively wrapped sell far better. We can't afford to fall behind our competitors in the way we present our goods for sale, or we won't sell enough to stay in business.

Another point I should like to make is that it costs the manufacturer almost as much to collect used bottles as to buy new ones, and it is far less convenient. I can assure you that we do not want to destroy the environment or use up all the world's raw materials any more than Mrs Holt does, but our first concern has to be the manufacture and sale of our products.

We have a research department, but our scientists can't afford to spend their time working

out ways of recycling the waste packaging from our products—that's a problem that needs to be dealt with at higher levels. In fact, it's beginning to look as if the rapidly rising cost of raw materials is going to force all manufacturers to reduce the amount of packaging they use, but the public will have to accept this without complaining.

It really is not fair to blame manufacturers for the problems that arise from trying to give the customer what he wants. Perhaps members of the public need re-educating, but that is not our job. It is one for the government and the schools. As for the wider problems of the growing shortage of raw materials, these must be dealt with by scientists and technologists at national and international levels.

A research scientist

There are no easy solutions to the problems caused by the shortage of raw materials, but I think we can he hopeful about some of the developments in recycling that are taking place. Several British newspapers are already being printed on recycled paper, and salvaged paper

has long been used for making cardboard boxes.

The technology involved in this is fairly simple, but some interesting new processes have been developed recently. Paper can now be eaten! It is softened and sweetened in a special machine and then fed to cows. In fact, it has been found that cows fed on cardboard boxes give a particularly creamy milk. Unfortunately the human stomach is very different from a cow's, so it seems unlikely that we shall ever be able to read *The Times* at breakfast one day and eat it for breakfast the next, but stranger things are possible.

Other waste products that Mrs Holt didn't mention, used motor car tyres for example, can also be recycled. Modern technology has found a way of producing half a ton of oil from one ton of used car tyres, and also a solid fuel even better than coal. Scientists and technologists in many countries are busy finding new ways of using our old rubbish. It now seems that there is some hope that we shall not run out of raw materials or ruin the countryside with rubbish dumps as Mrs Holt fears. I hope she finds these examples encouraging.

NOTES
timber wood
sliced cut (bread, meat etc.) into thin pieces for eating
carton small container
polythene plastic sheet used for wrapping food, etc.
recycle to make waste materials into new, useful products
salvage save from being wasted
incinerator closed fire for burning waste materials
spokesman person who speaks officially

scrap (of metal etc.) unwanted
extract take out
it's all very well it is easy but mistaken
research search for facts; *market research—* discovering what the public will buy
process (**n** & **v**) treat (eg food) with special machines or special substances

EXERCISES

Comprehension

1 What does Mrs Holt find difficult to understand?
2 How does she think the following can help to save raw materials *a* manufacturers?; *b* housewives?; *c* shops?; *d* local councils?; *e* the government?.
3 What reason does the government spokesman give for not doing more? What is the government already doing?
4 What reason does the representative from a food manufacturer give for *a* wrapping goods expensively; *b* not collecting used bottles?
5 What hopeful developments does the research scientist speak about?

Match the saying with the statement

Prevention is better than cure	The price of raw materials has risen; we have had a bad harvest and we have had a serious earthquake.
It never rains but it pours	We might never have discovered that cows produce good milk when fed on cardboard, if there hadn't been a shortage of cattle food.
Actions speak louder than words	We should enjoy our raw materials while we have them, and not worry about the future.
Necessity is the mother of invention	The government should supply money for collecting tin and paper and not just offer encouragement.
Live now, pay later	It is better to stop manufacturers wasting valuable raw materials than try to salvage them from rubbish.

Use of English

Part 1
Complete the following passage using one of the following:
   down   out   up

When I sorted ___ my rubbish, I found it contained a lot of paper and tin. I had read that world supplies of raw materials were being used ___ and that the price of goods could be brought ___ if paper and tin were recycled. We suggested this to our local council, but they turned ___ our proposal. They said that experiments elsewhere had turned ___ too expensive because of the cost of collections.

Part 2
Replace each phrasal verb above with one of the following:
   exhaust   prove   reject   empty   reduce

Vocabulary

Complete the following using the words given:
bar, bottle, box, can, carton, jar, packet, tin, tube
Example A ___ of cigarettes
Answer A packet of cigarettes

a ___ of toothpaste	a ___ of cream
a ___ of soap	a ___ of matches
a ___ of soap-powder	a ___ of chocolate
a ___ of beer	a ___ of milk
a ___ of jam	a ___ of fish

Discussion

What can be done about the growing shortage of raw materials?
Can you suggest other ways of recycling waste?

PROBLEMS? WORRIES? DIFFICULTIES?

Is there a simple answer to today's problems? I've just returned from the International Women's Conference in New York. It's surprising how similar problems are from country to country, but some of our sisters from the developing countries thought that we in the West were suffering from the changes that have taken place in our society over the last fifty years. Didn't most of the problems I tried to solve on my page—loneliness, divorce, insecurity—result from the breakdown of family life? Shouldn't I try to persuade my readers to return to the ways of the past?

I could not give a simple answer. Although I believe that every individual needs the security of a happy family life, I do not think it is possible to return to the pattern of life our grandparents knew—and that is still found in other parts of the world. Important social and economic changes have taken place which cannot be reversed. In Britain now, families are small and cannot satisfy all the needs of the individual. People's jobs or their studies take them far from home and they make new friends, friends who may come from completely different backgrounds. This makes life interesting, but it also involves certain risks.

For women, especially, modern life brings more opportunities and more problems. Now that they have smaller families and labour-saving devices why should women stay at home if they feel bored and want to take jobs? Why shouldn't they have equal rights with men to education and a career? Indeed the subject of equal rights was one of the main concerns of the International Women's Conference. But in our search for equal rights we must not forget our families. Mothers who go out to work have to make sure their children don't suffer. If a family cannot look after their old people themselves, then they must help them to be independent, or arrange for them to be cared for in homes.

We cannot turn the clock back. We must find new ways of caring for each other and organise our lives as intelligently and unselfishly as possible.

IMPOSSIBLE MOTHER-IN-LAW

My husband, our two teenage children and I live in a small three-bedroomed house. A year ago my husband invited his mother to come and live with us. Since then my life has been a misery and I sometimes wish I were dead. My mother-in-law criticises the children all the time and is never satisfied with anything I do for her. She can't find anything good to say about the younger generation. If she doesn't change her ways, I think I'll run away.

Don't do that! Why not discuss her with your husband instead? Explain your feelings to him, and say quite firmly that unless his mother behaves better she will have to leave. Although I believe it is good for old people to live with their families where possible, the situation in your home sounds impossible. There are excellent homes for the elderly, and she may be much happier in one of these.

HE NEEDS A SLAVE

I am forty-five and my children have grown up and left home. My husband works long hours and when he returns in the evening he just wants to watch TV—he never speaks to me. Not long ago I became so bored and depressed that I took the advice of my doctor and found a part-time job. My husband is furious. He now complains that I neglect

I'm here to help
says Jane Banks

him, and accuses me of being in love with my boss, which is nonsense. He insists that I give up my job, but I know that if I agree he will continue to behave as before.

Your husband seems to need a slave who will look after him without making any demands. His jealousy suggests that he is also very unsure of himself. In cases like this I think it is best to avoid a quarrel and instead try to win his sympathy. Keep telling him that you love him and explain how miserable you are at home all day. If this doesn't work then you should be firm and continue working. He will soon realise that he can't bully you and will come to accept the situation.

MUM WON'T LET ME LEAVE HOME

I am seventeen years old and leave school this year. A girl-friend is looking for a flat in London and wants me to share it with her. I think I would be able to find a job as a typist, but my mother won't allow me to leave home. She says I might be lonely and get into bad company. How can I persuade her to change her mind?

I wonder if you realise how expensive life in London is! I doubt whether you and your friend would earn enough to pay for a comfortable flat in a nice part of London. You would have to live in the suburbs and then you would need to spend a lot on fares. Your

mother might be happier if you lived in a YWCA hostel. You would make lots of friends, and there would be older people to keep an eye on you. If she agrees to let you go, you must fix up a job before you leave home. If your mother sees you're making sensible plans, she may change her mind.

WHAT WILL THE NEIGHBOURS SAY?

My daughter has suddenly returned from college and told us she is expecting a baby. Her father and I are shattered. We brought her up with great care and we keep asking ourselves where we went wrong. She says she doesn't intend to marry the baby's father as she doesn't love him. It seems she met him at a party and had too much to drink. We don't want her to come home as we live in a small village and there will be a lot of gossip. If she leaves college in the middle of term her teachers and friends will want to know why. I am very worried that people we know will find out the truth. How can we prevent this?

You can't. Even if your daughter managed to find somewhere to hide, there would still be talk. Better to face the neighbours and the gossip—but you may be surprised how much kindness and understanding you'll meet. Also your daughter should be with you at this time. She needs your help and support now, more than ever before.

You must help her decide what is best for the child and best for herself. I'm sending you some information about adoption societies, but if she wants to keep the baby, make sure she finishes her studies somehow. Could you look after the child for a year or so until your daughter qualifies? Perhaps the college will give her a year off? Once you have overcome your shock at this news I am sure you will find the strength to help your daughter make the right decisions, so that none of you will have any regrets in the future.

MAINLY FOR MEN
Our new feature for the men of the family

NOBODY LOVES ME

When I was sixteen I asked a girl out and she just laughed and said, 'No'. Since then I've been frightened to ask another girl out. I don't think I shall ever find someone to love me. I'm eighteen now and feel desperate. What can I do?

Every man is refused some time, you know—you were just unlucky that it happened the first time you asked a girl out. Try talking to a girl in a friendly way first, admire her clothes, ask her opinions, but above all take your time. If you're refused again, learn from it, but go on trying.

SHOULD I GO TO UNIVERSITY?

My father died five years ago and since then my mother has worked very hard to support us both. I am about to take A levels and my teachers expect me to do very well. They have suggested that I should go to university and my mother is very eager for me to do so. I have always wanted to be a teacher, but my mother has had such a hard life that I think it would be better for me to start earning a living. She could then give up her job and enjoy life a bit. What do you think?

I think your mother has a very nice son! It sounds as if you would make her very happy by going to university. If you take a job now you may never forgive yourself for sacrificing the opportunity to study. By training for a profession you will be in a better position to help your mother later, when she can no longer work. In any case you should get a good government grant which will certainly lighten your mother's financial burden. Good luck!

CHILDREN NEED THEIR FATHER TOO

Two years ago my wife left me and our two sons and went to live with another man. Since then I have managed to keep the home going with the help of my mother who lives nearby. My wife now says she wants a divorce. She's planning to marry her boyfriend and wants the children to live with her. She has already made me and the children very unhappy, and if she now takes them away from me, my life will be ruined. Surely children need their father too? Can you help me?

I think you will have to share the children with your wife, but do try not to fight over them. Whatever your feelings about her, the truth is that children need both a mother and a father. Nowadays the courts give custody of the children to the parent who can offer the most secure, loving home. They will see that you've cared for them very well during the last two years and I think you can be fairly optimistic about keeping them.

NOTES

divorce to end a marriage between a husband and wife
reverse turn backwards
device invention (machine etc.) *labour saving device* machines that do work for you
turn the clock back to replace modern ideas with old fashioned ones
bored tired because not interested
furious very angry
bully force to obey

fare money paid for a trip by bus, train, etc.
YWCA hostel hotel-like home provided by the Young Women's Christian Association
gossip (unkind) talk about other people
feature a special article in a newspaper
A levels exams that have to be taken before going to University in Britain (A = advanced)
custody right to look after
grant money awarded to a person to continue studies
burden heavy load or worry

EXERCISES

Comprehension

According to Jane Banks, which of these statements are true and which false?

1 There is a simple answer to today's problems.
2 Developed and developing countries have exactly the same social problems.
3 A happy family life is of no help to the individual in today's world.
4 It is wrong for families to put their old people in special homes.
5 Women should have equal rights with men to education and a career.
6 British couples should have larger families.
7 In the West people's jobs take them away from home.
8 It is a bad thing to have friends from different backgrounds.
9 Labour-saving devices make life easier for the housewife.
10 We should look forward, not back to the past.

Use of English

If he apologises, you should forgive him.
Write 10 sentences from these series of words using this pattern. Make all the changes and additions necessary to produce 10 correct sentences.

1 If/your parents/want/be/independent/you/help/them
2 If/your mother/ask/stay/you/let/her
3 She/tell/her husband/if/she/be/unhappy
4 He/tell/her/go/if/she/not behave/better
5 If/he/not agree/you/be/firm
6 If/your mother/let/you/go/you/stay/in/YWCA
7 She/continue/her studies/if/she/can
8 If/he/want/help/his mother/he/go/university
9 You/let/your wife/see/children/if/she/want/to
10 If/a girl/refuse/you/you/ask/another

Guided composition

Here is Jane Banks' answer to a letter received from a seventeen-year-old college student. Write *a* the conversation the girl had with her father when she came home late, and *b* the letter she wrote to Jane Banks. Jane Banks's reply:

Dear Sylvia,
I think you would be very foolish to leave home for such a silly reason particularly as this would mean leaving college too. I'm afraid I must agree with your father. Twelve o'clock seems a sensible time to come home at, and there is no reason why you should be allowed to do exactly what your friends do. By telling your father you want to leave home immediately, you will have hurt him, and naturally he is angry. Since he is paying for your course and supporting you, he has a right to expect you to keep his rules. My advice is to apologise and be patient.

Sincere good wishes,
Jane Banks

Vocabulary

Complete this passage by putting the words in brackets in a suitable form.
I had known him for four years and it seemed he had no 1 (*intend*) of marrying me. I desperately wanted 2 (*secure*) and to escape from my 3 (*lonely*). When I became friendly with another man, he showed such 4 (*jealous*) that I began to feel he really loved me. We married a year ago. He goes out a lot and I find my 5 (*suburbs*) life very boring. I would like to get a university 6 (*educate*) so that I can be independent.

Discussion

What do you consider are the main problems in family life today?
Is a woman's life today more difficult than in the past?

COMPUTERS

When Charles Babbage, a professor of mathematics at Cambridge University, invented the first calculating machine in 1812 he could hardly have imagined the situation we find ourselves in today. Nearly everything we do in the modern world is helped, or even controlled, by computers, the complicated descendants of his simple machine. Computers are being used more and more extensively in the world today, for the simple reason that they are far more efficient than human beings. They have much better memories and can store huge amounts of information, and they can do calculations in a fraction of the time taken by a human mathematician. No man alive can do 500,000 sums in one second, but an advanced computer can. In fact, computers can do many of the things we do, but faster and better. They can pay wages, reserve seats on planes, control machines in factories, work out tomorrow's weather, and even play chess, write poetry, or compose music. Let's look now at some of the ways in which computers concern people in their daily lives and work.

Computers and our cash

Mr Woods, a bank manager, discusses some of the ways in which computers control our cash. 'I think most of our customers realise that in modern banking we make extensive use of computers. They see that the codes on their cheques are printed in a special way so that they can be read by a computer—computers only seem to like rather square figures. And when they call in at the bank to find out the balance of their accounts, the clerk no longer shows them a big book with hand-written entries. Instead he goes and gets a print-out from the computer which records all the details of cash or cheques paid into or drawn out of customers' accounts. The day may soon come when we no longer need to carry cash around with us, or even a cheque book. The computer where we work will tell our bank computer how much our salary or wages are—and the government computer how much tax we should pay! Then when we go shopping we will just show a special card at the check-out point. The code on the card will be fed into the shop computer which will check with the bank computer that there is enough money in our account to pay for the goods we want, and that the card has not been stolen. If all is well the codes from the different items will be fed into the computer and the sum owing will be drawn from our account, but only 'on computer'. No money will ever change hands. Computerised shopping, like computerised banking, will be quick, safe and convenient.'

Computers and our health

Nurse Penny Atkins works in a large, modern hospital.
'We use computers a lot in medicine nowadays. For instance, at the hospital where I work we make patients' appointments through a computer, which saves a lot of time. So does keeping patients' records on a computer. It also saves space because you can get so much more information on to a piece of computer tape than a piece of paper. Another advantage is that anyone who wants information on a patient can get it quickly, or even at the same time as someone else. You just dial the computer. In the past a doctor might take a patient's records away to his room and keep them for weeks, which could make

CONCERN YOU

things difficult for the rest of us! Actually, computers can often do a doctor's work better than a human being can. Computers don't suffer from lack of sleep, so they don't miss important points. And because they never forget anything they've ever been told they're often better at working out what's wrong with a patient, or the best treatment to give him. Some people even think we should all have regular computer checks on our health and then we would be able to cure most diseases in the early stages. We'd all spend less time in hospital, so the future would be better for us over-worked nurses!'

Computers catch criminals

Chief Inspector Harston talks about ways in which computers can help the police fight crime.

'Members of the public often think of detective work as fast and exciting when most of it is slow and boring. For example, a detective on a stolen car case may have to check through long lists of information, and in the time it takes him to do this the thief may well escape. With the new National Police Computer we are now able to find out details of car ownership and driving licences in a fraction of the time it takes by traditional methods. We are also developing systems of storing fingerprint information in computers and even information about people's appearance. It's possible to work out codes for visual details and to link a computer with a videotape recorder (VTR). Then, instead of looking through books of photographs we'll be able to ask the computer to sort out the right ones, and see photographs of suspects flashed across a VTR screen. In police work speed is often essential, so computers are ideal for helping

us catch criminals. The only problem is that we now have a new kind of criminal—the very clever man who knows how to make huge sums of money by cheating a computer, and he is very difficult indeed to catch.'

Computers serve the arts

Mary Watts, a university librarian, points out that computers serve the arts as well as the sciences.

'I think many people associate computers with the world of science and maths, but they are also a great help to scholars in other subjects, in history, literature and so on. It's now possible for a scholar to find a book or article he needs very quickly, which, when a million or more new books are published each year, is quite an advantage. There's a system, controlled by computer, of giving books a code number, reducing them in size by putting them on microfiche, and then storing 3,000 or more in a container no bigger than a washing machine. You tell the computer which subject you're interested in and it produces any microfiche you need in seconds. It's rather like going to an expert who has read all the works on your subject and can remember where to find the correct information, which few human experts can! There are also systems being developed to translate articles from foreign magazines by computer, and to make up the many lists of information that are needed in a modern library. So computers can help us to deal with the knowledge explosion in many ways. I can imagine a time when libraries will be run by computers, without any human beings at all. If that happens in my lifetime I hope there'll be a computer somewhere that can find me another job!'

Computers make marriages

Computers can even control our love lives, as the following advertisement shows.

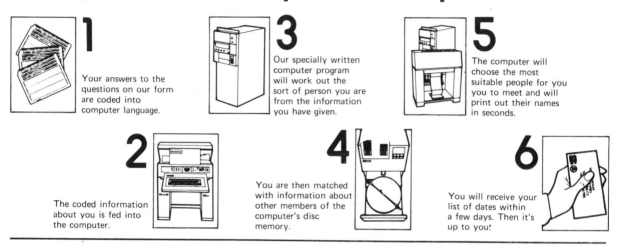

Find your perfect partner the fast efficient way – by computer

6 steps to friendship, with Compute-a-date

1 Your answers to the questions on our form are coded into computer language.

2 The coded information about you is fed into the computer.

3 Our specially written computer program will work out the sort of person you are from the information you have given.

4 You are then matched with information about other members of the computer's disc memory.

5 The computer will choose the most suitable people for you you to meet and will print out their names in seconds.

6 You will receive your list of dates within a few days. Then it's up to you!

Well, computers certainly concern people, so much so that perhaps people should be concerned about the growing power of computers. Will they come to control us completely? David Till, a computer expert, has the last word. 'Computers do work extremely fast, and may seem very clever to us, but in fact they can only do what they're told. *We* tell them what to do. Human beings are needed to program computers, and computers are only as good as the program fed into them. It's up to us to decide what we want to use computers for. They are our servants, and not our masters—yet.'

'I'll never understand what that stupid machine saw in you.'

NOTES
fraction a small amount
sum calculation
chess game played on a board of 64 squares by two people with 16 'men' each, the winner making it impossible for the other to move his 'king'
cash money in coins and notes
code a system of secret words, letters, numbers etc.
patient person receiving treatment from a doctor
dial to call by pressing keys etc.

visual able to be seen
link join
driving licence paper proving one is permitted to drive a car
videotape tape that records television sound and pictures
scholar learned person
microfiche page(s) of book(s) reduced to a very small size
date arranged meeting of man and woman

EXERCISES

Comprehension and discussion

1 Give three reasons why computers are being used.

2 How can computers help the following people in their work *a* employers?; *b* scholars?; *c* policemen?; *d* hospital workers?.

3 What possible disadvantages can computers have?

4 Do you know of other ways in which computers are being used?

5 Can you suggest ways in which they may be used in the future?

Guided summary

How does a computer work?
Here is a list of facts about computers. Choose the 5 main points that explain how a computer works and write them out in the correct order. Ignore facts that are not connected with the theme.

1 The computer stores information in its memory bank

2 A computer can do 500,000 sums in one second

3 Information is coded and prepared for the computer

4 Computers can be cheated

5 When information is needed a code is dialled

6 Computers help us to catch thieves

7 Information is fed into the computer

8 The computer then gives a print-out

Use of English

Changing habits
Part 1   used to for habits in the past
Example In the past I met my girlfriends at dances, but now . . .
Answer I used to meet my girlfriends at dances, but now . . .
These people are describing how computers have changed their working lives. Make 8 new sentences emphasising that their lives are now different, by using *used to*

1 Bank clerk: In the past we kept records in big heavy books, but now we keep them on computer tape.

2 Policeman: . . . I spent a lot of time checking through lists of information but now I get my information from the computer.

3 Nurse. . . . I wasted time looking for patient's records, but now I have them on computer.

4 Librarians: . . . we wasted a lot of space storing hundreds of books, but now we keep the contents on microfilm.

5 Criminal . . . I robbed banks and offices, but now I cheat computers.

6 Research scientist. . . . I had to make many different calculations, but now I feed the information into a computer.

Part 2   instead of   +—ing   changing from one habit to another
Example In the past I met my girlfriends at dances, but now I meet them by computer.
Answer Instead of meeting my girlfriends at dances, I meet them by computer.
Using the information in the 6 sentences above, make 6 new sentences with *instead of*

Part 3   no longer   +Present Tense   instead—followed by subject
Example In the past I met my girlfriends at dances, but now I meet them by computer
Answer I no longer meet my girlfriends at dances. Instead I meet them by computer
Make 12 new sentences using this pattern

Vocabulary

Re-arrange Column B so that each phrase is opposite the one in Column A that it explains:

Column A	Column B
a code	a game for two players
a fraction	a written account of facts
a computer	a piece of writing
a record	a small part
chess	a calculating machine
an article	a system of signs

Discussion

What's your view on computer dating?

HENRY MOORE
on his life and work

Henry Moore, the great British sculptor, was born in the little industrial town of Castleford in Yorkshire in 1898, the seventh child of his parents. From an early age he showed a deep interest in art and a feeling for shape and form.

'As boys we used to play in the claypits belonging to Castleford Pottery and make sculptures with the clay. It was so beautifully easy to shape.'

'When I was about eleven I heard my Sunday school teacher tell about the great sculptor, Michelangelo, which made me say that when I grew up I was going to be a great sculptor.'

'I could recognise the girls in the school by the shape of their legs. If their bodies and faces had been hidden by a board below which only their legs showed from the knees down, I could still have given a name to each pair.'

At the age of eleven he won a scholarship to Castleford Grammar School, where he developed his interest and abilities in art.

'There were three of us, all roughly the same age, competing for any art jobs that might be going in the Grammar School, like designing the cover of the school magazine, or costumes for the school play.'

He was determined to become an artist but his father had different views.

'My father was very sensible, and although he did not know much about the art world, he knew enough to realise that an artist's life was likely to be an awful struggle. And so, when I was 14 or 15, he advised me to carry on with my education and become a qualified teacher like my brothers and sisters. His point was that after I had a secure living I could then paint and do the sculpture I wanted.'

But after service in the 1914–18 war Moore was able, with the help of scholarships, to study art. Sadly, his father did not live to see his son's success as a sculptor, but died in 1922.

Of his mother Moore says:

'My mother had no knowledge of art. Like many parents she thought that whatever I did was very good. That was her attitude, except that one day I remember her saying, while she was watching me carving a big piece of stone, that she wondered why, when I'd been to Grammar School, I should have chosen such a hard physical job.'

Moore says of himself as a sculptor:

'The whole of my development as a sculptor is an attempt to understand and realise more completely what form and shape are about, and in my work I have tried to show an understanding of form in life, in the human figure, and in past sculpture. This is something that can't be learned

Left *the reclining figure outside the* UNESCO *building, Paris,* below *Moore in his studio working on a maquette*

in a day, for sculpture is a never-ending discovery. I have seen a great deal of the sculpture of the past. I think about sculpture all the time. I work at it in my studio for ten to twelve hours a day. I even dream about it.'

During his working life Moore has produced hundreds of drawings and sculptures, but certain themes occur again and again.

'From very early on I have had an obsession with the Mother and Child theme. It has been a universal theme from the beginning of time and some of the earliest sculptures we've found are of a Mother and Child. I discovered when drawing I could turn every little mark into a Mother and Child.'

In 1943 Moore was asked to carve a Madonna and Child for the church of St Matthew in Northampton, but was very doubtful about accepting this commission.

'It was one of the most difficult and heart-searching sculptures that I ever tried to do. I realised that I should not do an ordinary Mother and Child, put it in a church and call it a Madonna and Child. I felt uncertain whether I could really produce a piece of sculpture that I would be sure in my own conscience, in my own heart, was suitable. One problem lay in trying to make the child an intellectual-looking child, that you could believe might have more of a future than just an ordinary baby.'

Another favourite theme, perhaps reflecting Moore's pleasure in family life, is that of the Family Group.

'This plaster detail of the Tate *Family Group* shows the arms of the mother and father with the child forming a knot between them, tying the three into a family unity.'

But perhaps the most famous theme in Moore's work is that of the 'reclining figure'. In 1956 Moore was commissioned to produce a sculpture to go in front of the new UNESCO headquarters in Paris. His final choice was a reclining figure.

'I was using my own subject matter. I was doing what I would have done anyway, except I made it larger to make the correct scale for the architecture and its surroundings. It was the first big stone sculpture that I had done since the *Madonna and Child*.'

The final sculpture is 16 feet long. First Moore made a six inch maquette, and then a plaster working model one eighth of the final size. This was sent to Italy where he carved the final sculpture from Roman travertine marble.

'Roman travertine marble is a stone that I have loved since I first used it in 1932. I like its colour and its rough, broken, pitted surface. I am quite satisfied that the sculpture is the right size, scale and material for the building.'

Moore's ideas come from many sources.

'I find that all natural forms are a source of

unending interest—tree trunks, the growth of branches from the trunk, the texture and variety of grasses, the shape of shells, of pebbles... The whole of Nature is an endless source of examples of shape and form.'

Moore collects bones, shells, pebbles and pieces of wood, which he keeps in his studio.

'The variety of objects in my small studio provides me with many new ideas simply by looking at and handling them.'

Moore has described how one of his works came into existence.

'The *King and Queen* is rather strange. I can't explain exactly how it developed. Anything can start me off on a sculpture idea and in this case it was playing with a small piece of modelling wax. While I was playing with a piece of this wax it began to look like a horned Pan-like bearded head. Then it grew a crown and I recognised it immediately as the head of a king. I continued and gave it a body. When wax hardens it is almost as strong as metal. I used this special strength to repeat in the body the sense of royalty I found in the head. Then I added a second figure to it and it became a King and Queen. I realise now that it was because I was reading stories to Mary, my six-year-old daughter, every night, and most of them were about kings and queens and princesses. One of these sculptures went to Scotland, and is beautifully placed by its owner, Tony Keswick, in a moorland landscape. I think he rather likes the idea of the *King and Queen* looking from Scotland across to England.'

Right *a family group in bronze*

Moore's wife, Irina, has made the garden of their home, Hoglands, in Hertfordshire, into an ideal setting for his sculpture.

'Without that piece of land I cannot imagine how I could have produced some of the large sculptures that I have done in the last ten years. If a large sculpture had to be made in a studio it would be impossible to get away from it, and I would tend to work on its surface rather than on its bigger architectural forms. In our garden I can place the sculptures and see what they look like from a distance and in all weather conditions.'

Moore keeps some of his works in the garden at Hoglands. He tells this story about one of them:

'*Man*, who sits alone at the end of my garden, began as a detail for the Tate "Family Group". Later I used him as an experiment in casting in concrete. I found the material rather unsympathetic and so I faked him to look like bronze. The only people who were taken in were some local gypsies, who one night rolled all fifteen hundredweight of him a good hundred yards to the fence before one, more suspicious than the rest, struck him with a hammer and discovered not scrap metal but concrete. As I have said so often you should never judge sculpture at first sight.'

'Man' in the garden of Moore's home in Hertfordshire

NOTES

claypits place where clay (for making pots) is dug out of the ground
pottery place for making cups, saucers, plates etc.
scholarship money given to help a clever young person to continue his or her education
grammar school (formerly) school for pupils of age 11–18, perhaps leading to university entrance
costume dress especially as used in the theatre
physical of or concerning the body
theme subject, central idea

obsession idea filling the mind
intellectual having special qualities of the mind
pitted with very many little holes
texture arrangement of parts in ways that we can see and our fingers can feel
pebble small round stone
Tate = the Tate Gallery in London (the main British gallery of modern art)
fake give a false appearance (to)
gypsy member of a people of eastern origin who lead wandering lives in Europe

EXERCISES

Comprehension

Which of these statements are true and which false?
1 Moore had no success at school
2 He thought the Child should look intellectual
3 He is very interested in the theme of family life
4 Moore's 'Madonna and Child' stands in front of UNESCO headquarters in Paris
5 He gets many of his ideas from nature
6 His 'King and Queen' was a carefully planned sculpture
7 His garden is an ideal setting for his work
8 He always works in a studio

Use of English

Combine the following pairs of sentences
Example I saw him. He was working in his garden
Answer I saw him working in his garden
1 They heard him. He was working in his studio.
2 His mother watched him. He was carving a piece of stone.
3 Someone saw the gypsies. They were rolling 'Man' away.
4 He felt the wax. It was going hard.
5 His father noticed him. He was playing with some clay.
6 I smelt it. The wax was melting in the heat.

Guided composition

Read the following summary of a conversation between a BBC interviewer and Henry Moore. Write out the conversation in the form of a dialogue.
Interviewer: Did you ever work with clay as a boy?
Moore: I used to play . . .
I began by asking him if he had ever worked with clay as a boy and he told me that he used to play in the Castleford Pottery clay pits and make sculptures from the clay there. I asked him when he had first realised he wanted to be a sculptor. He explained that he had made this decison on learning about Michelangelo. I inquired whether he had always been interested in shape and form, and he described how he could always recognise girls at school from the shape of their legs. I then asked him about his parents' attitude to their artistic son. He explained that his father had been very sensible, warning him that an artist's life would be difficult and advising him to become a qualified teacher. He said that his mother had been very encouraging, but had known nothing about art.

Vocabulary

Fill in each blank with a suitable form of the word in italics
1 The gypsies *suspected* something. They were ____
2 He finds it *satisfactory*. He is ____ with it
3 He *carved* something. He made a ____
4 He is *obsessed* with this theme. He has an ____ with it
5 His mother *knew* nothing of art. She had no ____ of art
6 He *sculpts*. He is a ____

Discussion

Is a secure job more important than doing what you want to do?

15

Relax and Live

It is commonly believed that only rich middle-aged businessmen suffer from stress. In fact anyone may become ill as a result of stress if they experience a lot of worry over a long period and their health is not particularly good. Stress can be a friend or an enemy: it can warn you that you are under too much pressure and should change your way of life. It can kill you if you don't notice the warning signals. Doctors agree that it is probably the biggest single cause of illness in the western world.

What does stress do to our bodies?

When we are very frightened and worried our bodies produce certain chemicals to help us fight what is troubling us. Unfortunately these chemicals produce the energy needed to run away fast from an object of fear, and in modern life that's often impossible. If we don't use up these chemicals, or if we produce too many of them, they may actually harm us. The parts of the body that are most affected by stress are the stomach, heart, skin, head and back. Stress can cause car accidents, heart attacks, and alcoholism, and may even drive people to suicide.

What causes stress in the first place?

Our living and working conditions may put us under stress. Overcrowding in large cities, traffic jams, competition for jobs, uncertainty about the future, any big change in our lives, may be stressful. Some British doctors have pointed out that one of Britain's worst flu waves came within weeks of the country changing to decimal coinage. Also if you have changed jobs or moved house in recent months you are more likely to fall ill than if you haven't. And more people commit suicide in times of inflation.

What can we do about stress?

As with all illnesses prevention is better than cure. A very common danger signal is the inability to relax. 'When you're taking work home, when you can't enjoy an evening with friends, when you haven't time for outdoor exercise—that is the time to stop and ask yourself whether your present life really suits you,' says one family doctor. 'Then it's time to join a relaxation class, or take up dancing, painting or gardening.'

Stress—disaster or warning signal?
It depends on you, as the following three case studies show

James Taylor—a student—woke up at 2 am after sleeping badly and discovered that his body was covered in red lumps. He had never suffered from anything like this before, but being a final-year medical student, he knew the likely cause. Suddenly, for the first time in his life, two major stresses had occurred at the same time. He was under great pressure preparing for his exams and the girl he was in love with had just left him. Fortunately he was able to see the funny side of the situation and his sense of humour helped him to recover. Of course, most people would not be as knowledgeable as he was, and would be more frightened by the appearance of red lumps!

Sarah Lawson, a young mother, had two small children under five. She had recently moved to the suburbs of a small town in southern England. Her husband was often away on business and she had to manage the children and home on her own. Six months after she'd moved she developed a bad headache which lasted for twenty-four hours. 'I just didn't know what to do. Finally I phoned the doctor who came round immediately and gave me something to take away the pain. A week later I became terrified at the thought of going out to do my shopping. I ordered everything I needed by phone and had it delivered. I knew I couldn't continue like this for ever, and the day came when I just had to go out —my son needed some new shoes. I dressed the children, picked up the car keys and burst into tears. Luckily my husband rang, realised that something was seriously wrong and rushed home from the other side of the country.' The doctor advised Sarah to have a complete break from the children. They were sent to her mother, and a social worker helped her to make some friends. Her husband considered changing his job, but this proved unnecessary since Sarah had now met other young mothers she could share her worries with.

After working fifteen years for a building firm, Bill Pearson was given the responsible position of area manager. He had to master a lot of new information and spend some of his evenings and weekends in different parts of the country. He didn't really like his job, but he owed money on his new house and he didn't want to disappoint his wife by giving up his new position. Bill had always been a quiet, home-loving man, but after a few months in the job his personality changed. He became bad-tempered, continually criticised his wife's cooking and complained of a pain in his stomach. But Bill Pearson was lucky. He managed to persuade his firm to give him his old job back. He began to enjoy life again and gradually recovered.

You can't always change your job of course, but there are plenty of ways you can help yourself to relax and enjoy life—and beat the enemy 'Stress'. Here's how some of our friends relax:

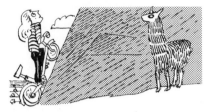

Penny Wheeler—doctor. 'When I feel I'm under stress I ride my bike up a very steep hill and then go home and fall asleep.'

John Hutchins—businessman. 'I get into a warm bath and lie there for an hour, listening to Mozart.'

Peter Matthews — lawyer. 'I get on with some rug-making. I work bright bold designs in wool and give the rugs to friends for Christmas.'

Peter Willis—teacher. 'I sometimes feel very tense in the evenings after school, so I phone a friend and have a long political argument with him. If he's not in, I record an argument on my tape-recorder, imagining what his replies would be.'

Mary Baker—newspaper reporter. 'I talk to my dog. He's very understanding. I tell him absolutely everything and experience a great sense of relief as he looks at me with his kind brown eyes.'

Ann Walker—secretary. 'I go shopping. The moment I walk into a shop all the pressures disappear— I become so interested in finding something nice. Recently, though, my bank refused to give me another cheque book because I was so overdrawn.'

A cheaper way for Ann Walker to relax, and for anyone else who suffers from tension and stress, is to do simple exercises regularly. You can do the exercises we suggest at home or even in the office!

Exercise 1   Standing

Purpose: To make waiting for a bus or standing in queues more bearable.

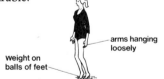

arms hanging loosely

Weight on balls of feet

Stand with your feet slightly apart, taking your weight on the balls of your feet. With your knees bent a fraction you can stand comfortably for quite a long time. Your shoulders should be back and down, with your arms hanging loosely.

Exercise 2   Sitting

Purpose: To rest the whole body and relieve tension, especially around the eyes.

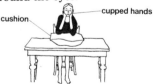

cushion — cupped hands

Sit well back in a chair so that the back of the chair supports the base of your spine. Place your elbows directly under your shoulders and support them on a cushion on a table. Then rest your cheek bones on your cupped hands. Keep your eyes closed. The longer you do this the better. Even one minute will help to relax tension.

Exercise 3   Lying

Purpose: Total relaxation: both as an excellent way of refreshing yourself during the day and also as an ideal preparation for sleep.

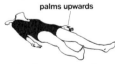

palms upwards

Lie on the floor, eyes closed, legs and feet fully relaxed, arms loosely out to the sides, palms upwards. Starting at the toes, think in turn of every part of the body, letting go completely and paying special attention to areas of particular tension.

NOTES
relax (v) be easy in mind and body **relaxation (n)**
alcoholism not being able to stop taking strong drink
(alcohol)
suicide killing oneself
decimal coinage system of money divided by tens and
hundreds

flu wave outbreak of influenza, a common fever
disaster sudden great misfortune, terrible happening
tense (adj) under pressure **tension (n)**
overdrawn having taken more money out of the
bank than one had in it
queue people waiting behind one another in a line

EXERCISES

Comprehension

Say which of the following are true and which
are false
1 Only middle-aged businessmen suffer from
  stress
2 Everyone who worries suffers from stress
3 Stress is caused by our running away from an
  object of fear
4 The stomach, heart, skin, head and back are
  often affected by stress
5 Many Britons committed suicide when their
  country changed to decimal coinage
6 If there is a lot of uncertainty in your life you are
  more likely to suffer from stress
7 Enjoyable hobbies help people to relax
8 Stress can be a warning signal

Use of English

Part 1
Suggest answers to each of the following problems
using the patterns in the table below.

Problems
1 I can't afford any new clothes.
2 All my muscles are tense.
3 I need a change of scene.
4 I have no pictures for my walls.
5 I'm getting fat.
6 I never go out in the evening.

Suggestions

Why don't you	take a holiday
If I were you I'd	learn to sew
I think you should	join a relaxation class
I suggest you	take up dancing
	take up painting
	do exercises every day

Part 2
Look at the pictures at the top of the facing page.
What advice would the following people give to
someone who could not relax.

1 Penny Wheeler: Why . . . . ride your
  bike . . . .
2 John Hutchins: If . . . . get into a
  warm bath . . . .
3 Peter Matthews: I think . . . . . . take up . . . . .
4 Ann Walker: I suggest you . . . .

Part 3
Make your own suggestions in response to the
following statements using the patterns you have
practised.

1 I hate living in an overcrowded city.
2 My girlfriend is making me very unhappy.
3 I don't know anyone in this town.
4 I have to work very long hours.

Invent more problems and make suitable
suggestions.

Guided summary

Complete this summary by filling in the gaps with
the correct prepositions.
  for under from by of after on
Young or old, rich or poor, anyone can suffer 1 __
stress. Doctors say we become ill 2 __ too much
worry. We can be 3 __ stress for many reasons.
Looking 4 __ children can make us tense.
Competition 5 __ jobs can also cause worry, and
living in the suburbs 6 __ a large town can be
very lonely. Both our bodies and minds are
affected 7 __ stress. Good health depends 8 __
getting enough exercise and relaxation.

Vocabulary

1 She was very *relieved*. She experienced a great
  sense of ____
2 He had a big *overdraft*. He was badly ____
3 They like *arguing*. They like an ____
4 Take a deep *breath*. ____ in deeply.
5 She was very *tense*. She was suffering from ____
6 He *enjoyed* his new life. He found it ____

Discussion

Do you ever feel tense? When?
How do you relax?

16

In films and fairy stories poor girls meet princes and poor boys find princesses. They fall in love at first sight, get married —often after a long struggle against wicked enemies—and live happily ever after. But what happens in real life? We talked to three happily-married couples and asked them how they'd met.

Husband and wife by airmail

'You must be mad,' his friends said, as thirty-year-old John Briggs of Hatfield left London Airport to fly to Brazil. John was going half-way round the world to meet a girl he'd never seen but hoped to marry. The trip was costing him three months' pay—in fact he'd had to borrow from his father and an aunt to buy his ticket— and he had no idea whether the pretty dark-haired girl he only knew from photographs and letters would even like him. 'I'd had a good life as a bachelor,' says John, four years later, his arm round his wife and their two lovely children, 'but I felt something was missing. I had a good job, my own house and plenty of friends. I'd had plenty of girlfriends too, but somehow no one ever seemed quite the right girl for me. Then one day I was looking through a magazine during my lunch hour when a photograph of a pretty girl caught my eye. It was part of an advertisement for a World Penfriends Circle. I decided to write off to them immediately. All my friends had a good laugh, I remember.'

John received the names of four girls, two from Japan, one from Finland, and one from Brazil, and wrote to all of them, enclosing a photograph of himself. The last to reply was Maria from Brazil, but it was Maria who came to take first place in John's heart. They wrote to each other for a year, Maria in Portuguese and John in English—all the letters had to be translated— and then one of Maria's uncles came to England on a business trip. Maria had asked him to arrange a meeting with John and report back to

Brazil on what her English penfriend was really like. The uncle said that John was 'a fat little fellow without much hair' but he must have said some nicer things too, for Maria's parents wrote to John inviting him to visit their family. John replied saying he'd love to.

A practical man, John started to get organised. As soon as he had the money for his air ticket he wrote to Maria asking her what her views on getting married were. He also sent an engagement ring, and a Valentine card every day! Maria wrote back to say they could decide whether to get married or not once they met—but she started making a wedding dress of beautiful white silk, just in case...

The day John was due to arrive Maria waited anxiously at the airport. Suppose he didn't like her? But when his plane came in she didn't even recognise him! Her uncle had to point him out. 'He was the man with the nicest smile,' says Maria, 'and he was just the right height for me!' They both realised immediately that they were just right for each other in lots of other ways too. Ten days later they were married and Maria came to live in England with her husband—'the best thing that's ever come to me through the post' she says.

Husband and wife for £45 each

Attractive Kay Knight is expecting her first baby in a few months' time. She smiled happily at her husband Mike as she told us their story. 'I woke up on my thirty-fifth birthday thinking,

"Help. I'm turning into a real old spinster schoolteacher". All my friends seemed to be married with homes and families of their own. But where was I? I love my job—don't get me wrong. I've had a very satisfying career, but teaching other people's children isn't the same as bringing up your own.' 'She'll make a wonderful mother,' said Mike. 'I can't think why she wasn't snapped up years ago. But I'm glad she wasn't, or I wouldn't have found her.'

How *did* they find each other? 'Well,' said Kay, 'as a young woman I'd had a few boyfriends, but never anything serious. Then I realised I wasn't even meeting any men, not unmarried ones anyway. So I took a deep breath and wrote to a Marriage Bureau.' Kay had to fill in a detailed form and then attend an interview. 'It was very thorough,' she said. 'They really wanted to make sure I was serious about wanting to get married, and they took a lot of trouble to find out what kind of person I was and the sort of man I thought I'd like to marry. I was told I'd be given three introductions to suitable men for a fee of £15. If I married one of them, I'd have to pay another £30.' The first introduction was to another teacher, which she didn't think was a good idea, but the second was to Mike.

Mike took up the story. 'I got married when I was a young man of 22, but my wife was killed a year later in a car accident. I was completely shattered. I put all my energies into my work and spent many years abroad with my firm. Then I came back to England to work at Head Office and realised how empty my life had become. I didn't just want work; I wanted a wife and children. I needed someone to make my house into a home. I wasn't interested in young girls, but how could I find a mature, loving woman to share my life? I think my sister and brother-in-law must have guessed how I was feeling. They introduced me to a charming older couple one evening. After they'd gone home I remarked how well-suited they seemed and my sister told me why—they'd met through a Marriage Bureau. 'You should give it a try,' she said. So I did.'

Mike phoned a bureau the very next day and went for an interview the following week. He was given three names, including Kay's. He wrote to her first because he thought a schoolteacher would probably like children. Their first date was a disaster. 'We agreed to meet for a picnic and it poured with rain,' he told us. 'But we both saw the funny side of it, and from then on everything went right.' Within a month of

✳✳

their first meeting he proposed and they got engaged. The wedding took place a year ago. 'Speaking as a businessman,' said Mike, 'this is the best deal I've ever made!'

Husband and wife by arrangement

Yoshio and Hiromi Tanaka are a young Japanese couple living in the USA while he studies electrical engineering. They clearly love each other very deeply, but, says Yoshio, 'We didn't marry for love in the Western sense. We got married in the time-honoured Japanese way. Our parents arranged our marriage through a matchmaker. In Japan we believe that marriage is something that affects the whole family, not just the young couple concerned. So we think it is very important to match people according to their social background, education and so on. Matchmakers are usually middle-aged women who keep lists of suitable young people with information about their families, education and interests. When our parents thought it was time for us to get married they went to a local matchmaker and asked her for some suggestions. We discussed the details and looked at the photos she sent, and then our parents asked her to arrange a "marriage interview" for the two of us.'

A Japanese marriage interview is held in a public place, such as a hotel or restaurant, and is attended by the boy and the girl, their parents and the matchmaker. Information about the couple and their families is exchanged over a cup of tea or a meal. Then the boy and the girl are left alone for a short time to get to know each other. When they return home they have to tell the matchmaker whether they want to meet again or not. If both of them want another meeting, the matchmaker arranges it, and after that they can decide to carry on the courtship themselves. Here Hiromi said with a gentle smile, 'Not so long ago, the girl could never refuse to go out again with a boy who liked her, but now she can. I thought Yoshio was really rather nice, so I didn't refuse.'

Yoshio continued: 'When our parents realised we were serious about each other, they started to make arrangements for our wedding. My family paid the "Yuino" money to Hiromi's. This is money to help pay for the wedding ceremony and for setting up house afterwards. We also gave her family a beautiful ornament to put in the best room of their house, so everyone knew that Hiromi was going to marry. Six months after our first meeting we were married. A traditional Japanese wedding is a wonderful ceremony, and our traditional custom of arranged marriages has given me a wonderful wife.'

Courtship customs

Did you know

that most British couples first meet at a dance?

that in some parts of Africa men pay for their wives with cows?

that in Germany you can advertise for a partner on television? India — newspaper

that in Britain girls can propose in Leap Year (1976, 1980 and every fourth year following)?

that in the USA boys and girls start dating very young, as young as 12.

NOTES

bachelor unmarried man
engagement ring ring given by a man to a woman to show a promise to marry her
Valentine card card expressing love, usually sent on 14 February, St Valentine's Day
spinster unmarried woman
get [me] wrong misunderstand [me]
snap up take eagerly

Marriage Bureau office which arranges marriages
interview formal meeting of two or more people
shatter break completely (in this case, psychologically)
mature having reached a state of full natural development
courtship meetings when a man tries to win a girl's love
traditional passing on of customs from parent to child

EXERCISES

Choose the best answer.
1 John's friends thought he was mad *a* to want to get married; *b* to want to marry a girl who wouldn't buy his ticket; *c* to want to marry a Brazilian girl; *d* to want to marry a girl he'd never met.
2 *a* John could easily afford the trip to Brazil; *b* John's employers were paying for the trip; *c* John's relations had bought the ticket for the trip; *d* John's relations were lending him the money for the trip.
3 Maria's uncle thought John was *a* particularly handsome; *b* too old for Maria; *c* rather a rich man; *d* rather fat and short.
4 'I was completely shattered.' This means that Mike was *a* badly injured; *b* very surprised; *c* deeply shocked; *d* very tired.
5 Mike Knight says 'I can't think why she wasn't snapped up years ago.' This means he doesn't understand why *a* she didn't try to get married years ago; *b* she didn't want to get married years ago; *c* someone didn't marry her quickly years ago; *d* she didn't get very bad-tempered.
6 Yoshio and Hiromi *a* have gone to live permanently in the USA; *b* were born in the USA; *c* are only staying in the USA until Yoshio finishes his course; *d* intend to stay in the USA

Use of English

Part 1   This is the best deal I've ever made
Make sentences like this from the following.
Example She/clever/girl/he/ever/work with.
Answer She's the cleverest girl he's ever worked with.
Say the sentences using the short forms where possible (*she's, I've*).
Write the sentences using the long forms (*she has, I have*).

1 He/handsome/man/she/ever/see
2 She/intelligent/girl/I/ever/speak to
3 This/anxious/day/we/ever/spend
4 That/nice/thing/you/ever/say
5 He/friendly/dog/they/ever/have
6 He/practical/man/she/ever/know

Part 2   I've never made a better deal
Using the information in the six sentences above make six new sentences with this pattern.
Example She's the cleverest girl he's ever worked with.
Answer He's never worked with a cleverer girl.

Guided summary

Connect the answers to these questions to make one paragraph about marriage by arrangement in Japan. The words in brackets are suggested links; for example in 3: They arrange a marriage interview, *which* is held in . . .
1 Who helps Japanese parents find suitable husbands and wives for their children?
2 What sort of people are matchmakers usually? (*and*) What do they keep?
3 What do they arrange? (*which*) Where is it held? (*and which*) Who is this attended by?
4 What do the families do at the interview? (*and then*) Are the boy and girl left alone, or not?
5 Do the young people have to meet again if they don't want to, or not?
6 What does the young man give the girl when they decide to marry?

Discussion

1 People would be happier if their marriages were arranged for them.
2 What possible problems can people have when they marry people from different backgrounds, countries or cultures?

A fashion of the 1970s seemed to be a move back to a simpler way of life. More and more young couples are leaving well-paid jobs in London and other cities to go and live in remote parts of the British Isles where they grow their own food, make their own clothes, and never watch TV.

They are not satisfied with the quality of life in twentieth century Britain, and are searching for something different. But they are not the first to flee modern Britain. More than ten years ago, some newcomers to Britain were very disappointed in what they found.

My friends the Tristan islanders

WHY DID THEY LEAVE US?

BY CHARLES YATES

Charles Yates is a reporter who lived on the remote island of Tristan da Cunha in the South Atlantic for a few months. When the islanders came to Britain he spent a lot of time observing them in their new life. Here is his report:

It is very difficult for us who live in an advanced technological society to understand the shock the islanders experienced when they came to Britain. In a few days they had moved suddenly into the twentieth century. Their whole life had been their small island with its green fields, stormy seas, cold mountains, cattle, sheep and dogs.

Disaster victims decide to return home

Officials had a shock yesterday. After only eighteen months of life in modern Britain, the Tristan islanders voted to return home.

The islanders were evacuated from Tristan da Cunha in October 1961 when their volcanic island suddenly erupted. They were brought to England by ship and given homes and jobs in Southampton. At that time no one imagined they would ever be able to return. The eruption was so severe it was thought their homes had been completely destroyed. Experts also feared that the volcano might erupt again.

An advance party that reached the island a few weeks ago was more optimistic. They reported that the damage was not as bad as suspected. The lava was still warm but the volcano seemed dormant again. Their chief worry was that they would be attacked by their dogs which had turned wild and killed a large number of sheep and cattle.

In spite of this favourable report, representatives of the Foreign Office were astonished that such a large majority (97%) should want to return. The islanders will face many hardships: landing on the island may in itself be very difficult. The main beach is covered in lava and most of the year bad weather conditions make it dangerous to approach the shore. The islanders' chief means of support, the fish canning factory, was destroyed and many of their homes were damaged. Nevertheless their present mood is one of joy and relief. As one young seaman remarked, 'There was no need to take a vote. They'd packed already.'

That life had been simple and uncomplicated, and the rush and noise of the twentieth century were indeed far away. Suddenly they were face to face with the 1960s—miniskirts, the twist, television in almost every home. For the first time in their lives they saw motor cars, buses, cinemas and theatres. Exciting for the young perhaps, but for the older generation the new way of life was more difficult. In my conversations with them it became clear that many missed their simple clothes, simple food and simple truths. In spite of the volcano they wanted to go home.

The following story shows the sort of problems the islanders met. A young girl went to see one of the officials at Calshott Camp. She knocked gently on his door. There was no reply. A friendly Englishman noticed her and called out: 'Ring the bell.' The girl looked puzzled. He went up to her and showed her the little button at the side of the door. 'Press that,' he said, and walked

Left lava *from the erupting volcano*

off. The girl looked fearfully at the button, took a deep breath and pressed it with her thumb. She waited and waited, her thumb firmly on the button. Suddenly the door flew open and an angry official stood there, shouting, 'What's all this about? You've been ringing that bell for five minutes. You'll deafen me.' The poor girl was so frightened that she nearly fell backwards down the steps. She hadn't realised she should take her thumb off! And the official realised, for the first time, how confusing life in Britain must be for the islanders. But there were many deeper problems. Before making their decision to return to Tristan, the islanders held endless discussions in their homes about the future. One evening I recorded the following:

YOUNG FATHER Can it be right for us to vote on the future of our children? If we return they won't be educated or trained for any special job.

HIS WIFE That's true, but I think our children were much happier on Tristan. There was always something useful for them to do. We needed their help and they had a real contribution to make. We had no problem of crime, and certainly no teenage crime.

THEIR DAUGHTER Life was quieter and slower. I felt free on Tristan.

ANOTHER GIRL Free in what way? You were free to die of appendicitis because there was no doctor on Tristan. I feel safer in England.

A YOUNG MAN On Tristan the whole family lived together or near each other. We certainly didn't send our old people to special homes.

OLD WOMAN But we old people get a pension in England and we can be independent. We're not a burden to our children and we don't have to work until the day we die.

OLD MAN Is a pension so important? What use is money? In England a man is judged by what he owns. On Tristan we judge a man by what he is and what he can do. Who is the quickest at shearing a sheep? Who is the best at collecting birds' eggs?

SINGLE WOMAN But it's so nice to have money in your pocket and to be able to spend it in the lovely shops here.

SINGLE MAN But it's all buying and selling in England. Everything has a price. If people help each other and share their goods you don't need money.

WIDOW Yes, it was much more friendly on Tristan. We saw so much of each other and we enjoyed each other's company. In England people don't realise how lonely they are.

What can we learn from this experience? We thought we had so much to offer, but the Tristan da Cunhans have made us think again about the quality of life in twentieth century Britain. In the words of the Reverend Neil Smith, a local priest who knew the islanders well:

'The people of Tristan da Cunha have reminded us that happiness does not lie in material possessions. It lies in personal relationships. They come from a small, close community where everyone knows everyone else. The population is, as it were, one large family, but a family where divorce is almost unknown, where quarrels are rare and where the old have an honoured place. No man or group of men is given special favours. There is no class war, because there are no classes. As the constitution of Tristan da Cunha, 1817, states: "No member shall assume any superiority whatever, but all are to be considered equal in every respect." Their economy is simple: farmers and fishermen, they live close to the soil and the sea. As Frances Repetto, an inhabitant of the island, wrote "Every person on Tristan can make his own living if he lives on his potatoes, looks ahead, and saves for a rainy day." We, in Britain, would do well to look at life on Tristan and consider the lessons it teaches us about the way ahead.'

So the Tristan islanders returned home, but that was not the end of the story. Some of them were unable to settle and came back to Britain again. Having tasted the pleasures of modern city life they were no longer content with the hard, simple life on their remote island. But they have never been really happy in twentieth century Britain either. There are no easy solutions to the problems of modern living, as those now choosing 'the simple life' may soon find.

NOTES

remote distant
flee run away (from)
disaster victim person who has suffered from a disaster
evacuate take out
dormant not active
mood feeling

twist a 1960s popular dance
appendicitis illness that is treated by cutting out the *appendix* a part that is no longer necessary
shear cut the wool of a sheep
assume superiority consider oneself better or more important than others
save for a rainy day provide something for possible future needs

EXERCISES

Comprehension

Choose the best answer in each of the following.

1 The islanders left Tristan because *a* life on the island was too hard; *b* their lives were in danger; *c* they wanted to see Britain; *d* they thought the volcano might erupt.

2 The older islanders *a* were happier in England than the younger islanders; *b* wanted bigger pensions; *c* missed their old life very much; *d* wanted to live in special homes.

3 The young girl pressed the button a long time because *a* she did not think it was working; *b* she did not realise it was a bell; *c* she did not know it was impolite to ring for so long; *d* she wanted someone to come quickly.

4 The islanders decided to go home because *a* they preferred their island way of life; *b* the Foreign Office wanted them to leave; *c* they did not like English food; *d* there were no jobs for them in England.

5 The island gets its name from *a* an Englishman; *b* a volcano; *c* its first inhabitant; *d* a Portuguese.

6 The experience of the Tristan islanders shows us that *a* most people prefer life in the country *b* life is much harder in Britain than on Tristan *c* life on Tristan is lonelier than life in Britain. *d* big changes make some people feel very unsettled.

Use of English

Make 7 true sentences from the following table taking care to match columns 1 and 3 according to meaning. Begin each sentence:

Most of the islanders { would rather
{ would prefer to...rather than...

1	2	3
grow their own food		have a job in a factory
work in the open		watch TV
live as one big family	than	shop in a supermarket
wear simple clothes		live alone
talk in the evenings		follow modern fashion
be surrounded by friends		live in modern society
lead a simple life		live among strangers

Guided summary

Taking your information from the islanders' conversation write two paragraphs (100–125 words) one for and one against staying in Britain (or your own country). Notes have been given to help you with the first paragraph.

For		Against	
1 better education/children		1	...
2 safer/doctors		2	...
3 old people/independent/pensions		3	...
4 enjoyable/buying things/beautiful shops		4	*etc.*

Vocabulary

Complete the following by putting the words in brackets in the correct form.
The islanders left Tristan in 1961 when there was a volcanic 1 (*erupt*) which caused a lot of 2 (*destroy*). Their lives on Tristan had not been very 3 (*complicate*) and they felt lost in an advanced 4 (*technology*) society. Although 5 (*office*) and neighbours were kind to them, certain things happened which 6 (*fright*) and 7 (*worry*) them. Before deciding to return they held endless 8 (*discuss*). Almost all of them agreed that 9 (*happy*) did not lie in material 10 (*possess*).

Discussion

Would you like to live on an island like Tristan da Cunha?

18 Alfred Nobel— a man of contrasts

Alfred Nobel, the great Swedish inventor and industrialist, was a man of many contrasts. He was the son of a bankrupt, but became a millionaire; a scientist with a love of literature, an industrialist who managed to remain an idealist. He made a fortune but lived a simple life, and although cheerful in company he was often sad in private. A lover of mankind, he never had a wife or family to love him; a patriotic son of his native land, he died alone on foreign soil. He invented a new explosive, dynamite, to improve the peacetime industries of mining and road building, but saw it used as a weapon of war to kill and injure his fellow men. During his useful life he often felt he was useless: 'Alfred Nobel,' he once wrote of himself, 'ought to have been put to death by a kind doctor as soon as, with a cry, he entered life.' World-famous for his works he was never personally well known, for throughout his life he avoided publicity. 'I do not see,' he once said, 'that I have deserved any fame and I have no taste for it,' but since his death, his name has brought fame and glory to others.

He was born in Stockholm on October 21, 1833 but moved to Russia with his parents in 1842, where his father, Immanuel, made a strong position for himself in the engineering industry. Immanuel Nobel invented the landmine and made a lot of money from government orders for it during the Crimean War, but went bankrupt soon after. Most of the family returned to Sweden in 1859, where Alfred rejoined them in 1863, beginning his own study of explosives in his father's laboratory. He had never been to school or university but had studied privately and by the time he was twenty was a skilful chemist and excellent linguist, speaking Swedish, Russian, German, French and English. Like his father, Alfred Nobel was imaginative and inventive, but he had better luck in business and showed more financial sense. He was quick to see industrial openings for his scientific inventions and built up over 80 companies in 20 different countries. Indeed his greatness lay in his outstanding

Dynamite used in a copper mine

ability to combine the qualities of an original scientist with those of a forward-looking industrialist.

But Nobel's main concern was never with making money or even with making scientific discoveries. Seldom happy, he was always searching for a meaning to life, and from his youth had taken a serious interest in literature and philosophy. Perhaps because he could not find ordinary human love—he never married—he came to care deeply about the whole of mankind. He was always generous to the poor: 'I'd rather take care of the stomachs of the living than the glory of the dead in the form of stone memorials,' he once said. His greatest wish, however, was to see an end to wars, and thus peace between nations, and he spent much time and money working for this cause until his death in Italy in 1896. His famous will, in which he left money to provide prizes for outstanding work in Physics, Chemistry, Physiology, Medicine, Literature and Peace, is a memorial to his interests and ideals. And so, the man who felt he should have died at birth is remembered and respected long after his death.

The Will

'...the whole of my remaining estate shall be dealt with in the following way: the capital shall be safely invested to form a fund. The interest on this fund shall be distributed annually in the form of prizes to those who, during the previous year shall have done work of the greatest use to mankind. The said interest shall be divided into 5 parts and distributed as follows: one part to the person who shall have made the most important discovery or invention within the field of Physics; one part to the person who shall have made the most important chemical discovery or improvement; one part to the person who shall have made the most important discovery within the field of physiology or medicine; one part to the person who shall have produced within the field of literature the most outstanding work of an idealistic tendency; and one part to the person who shall have done the most or the best work for brotherhood between nations, for the abolition or reduction of permanent armies and for the organization and encouragement of peace conferences. The prizes for physics and chemistry shall be awarded by the Swedish Academy of Sciences, that for medical works by the Caroline Institute in Stockholm, that for literature by the Academy in Stockholm, and that for workers for peace by a committee of five people to be elected by the Norwegian Parliament. It is my firm wish that in awarding the prizes no consideration whatever shall be given to the nationality of the candidates, but that the most worthy shall receive the prize, whether he be a Scandinavian or not.'

Paris, November 27, 1895

THE NOBEL MEDAL

FRONT

BACK

How a Nobel prizewinner is chosen

1 The Nobel Committees send invitations to hundreds of scientists and scholars around the world, asking them to suggest names for the Nobel prizes in the coming year.
2 The names are sent in by February 1.
3 Each committee, with the help of specially appointed experts, discusses the names suggested, and makes out a short list to present to the prize-awarding institution. A vote is taken for the final choice.
4 The names of the prizewinners are announced in October or November.
5 The prizes are awarded on December 10. The Peace Prize is presented at Oslo University, the others at a ceremony in Stockholm. The King of Sweden presents a diploma, a medal and a cheque to each prizewinner and there is a ceremonial dinner afterwards in the City Hall. Each Nobel prizewinner is expected to give a 'Nobel lecture'.

Some famous Nobel prizewinners

1911	**Marie Curie**	France	**Chemistry**	Discovery of radium
1921	**Albert Einstein**	Germany	**Physics**	Theory of relativity
1961	**Dag Hammarskjold**	Sweden	**Peace**	Work for the United Nations Organisation
1962	**Francis Crick** **James Watson** **Maurice Wilkins**	Britain USA USA	**Medicine**	Discovery of the structure DNA
1970	**Alexander Solzhenitsyn**	USSR	**Literature**	

NOTES
bankrupt person who cannot pay his debts
Crimean War (1853–6) Russia was against Turkey, Britain and France
estate property of a person who has died
distribute give out

abolition ending
candidate person who is being considered
diploma paper showing success
DNA *deoxyribonucleic acid,* found in the nucleus of every cell and considered as controlling the nature of development

EXERCISES

Comprehension

Say which of the following statements are
true or false.
1 Alfred Nobel was a great inventor
2 He expected dynamite would be used in mining
and road building
3 He spent all his youth in Sweden
4 His father invented the landmine
5 He married at an early age
6 He worked hard to end wars
7 He was a scientist and knew nothing about
literature
8 His will provides for prizes in physics, chemistry,
medicine, literature and peace

Use of English

From the notes below make six sentences about
Alfred Nobel, each showing he led a life of
contrasts. This will mean linking a statement
based on cues in Column A with another based
on cues in Column B, using *but* to form the link.
Example A. be/scientist   B. love/literature
Answer Nobel was a scientist, but he loved
literature

Column A	Column B
be/very rich indeed	never have/family of his own
be/happy among friends	see/invention used as an instrument of death and destruction
love/the whole human race	die/alone in a foreign land
love/own country	live/quite simply
live/useful life	be/sad when he was on his own
invent/dynamite for peaceful purposes	often feel/useless

Now write the sentences again beginning *Although*
Example A. be/scientist B. love/literature
Answer Although he was a scientist, he loved
literature.

Guided summary

In one paragraph summarise the life of Alfred
Nobel.

Points	*Suggested links*
When and where was Alfred Nobel born?	*but*
Where did his family move when he was 9?	
How old was he when his family returned to Sweden?	*and*
Where did he start work?	*where*
What did he study there?	
What other subjects was he also interested in?	
Was he a successful business man or not?	*and*
How many countries did he build up companies in?	
What did he care deeply about?	*and*
What was his greatest wish?	

Vocabulary

Complete these sentences by using a suitable form
of the word given.
Mark the stressed syllable on the new word, as, for
example, in the word *photógrapher*
1 He was a businessman who was also an (ideal)
2 Although he lived abroad for many years, he
remained (patriot)
3 His life was very (use), but he often felt (use)
4 He was one of Sweden's great (industry)
5 He was an excellent (language)

Discussion

Do the Nobel prizes cause more trouble than they
are worth? Should they be abolished?

19 The purest of human pleasures

'God almighty first planted a garden and, indeed, it is the purest of human pleasures.' FRANCIS BACON 1561–1621 *Of Gardens*

The first man and the first woman lived in the most beautiful garden the world has ever known, the Garden of Eden, but they angered God who had made the garden and were thrown out. Since then, man has multiplied and wandered to all parts of the world, but everywhere he has settled he has grown first food for his use and then plants for his pleasure. For centuries gardens have brought beauty and joy to kings in their castles and countrymen in their cottages. Today, even if people have no garden of their own, they can enjoy the beauty of public parks and share in the sights and scents of the many private gardens which are open to visitors.

There are many different kinds of gardens, from the few flowers round the smallest house in the country to the great historic gardens of French castles. They can be formal, with every plant carefully placed as part of a man-made design, or informal, looking as if every flower has sprung from seeds sown by nature. Perhaps the best example of an informal garden is the traditional English cottage garden.

English cottage gardens

The charming cottage garden has its roots in humble but not necessarily unhappy social conditions. Yet today it has risen to the height of fashion. The English cottage garden was created by people too poor in worldly goods to do much else than care for their own little piece of earth in the little spare time they had. But they must have been rich in love for plants and flowers. And they must have had a good eye for them too, for they were quick to notice any curious change in a plant and to care for it. Sometimes there would be a difference in leaf colouring, or the flowers may have been bigger or a new colour. They had to be preserved, reproduced, then

84

passed on to others. This is how new plants have become varieties with names of their own—like the famous Mrs Sinkins pink, named after the wife of the Slough workhouse keeper.

The cottage gardeners of the past had no fancy ideas about grouping plants in careful patterns. The result was that their gardens became a mass of flowers and foliage. The traditional cottage garden, with its fruit trees blossoming in spring and their branches heavy with the gifts of fruit in autumn, with its narrow paths winding between borders of sweet-scented flowers, with its gaily-coloured roses climbing along walls and over fences, and its neat rows of vegetables for the small but welcoming kitchen, has become an ideal with modern garden designers. But true cottage gardens cannot be designed. They must be allowed to grow, with plants given by friends

in one corner, cuttings begged from neighbours in another. They must welcome all newcomers and find a home for them, especially the self-sown flowers which often seem to spring up in just the right place to complete the colourful scene. No traditional plant should be turned away, for the essential spirit of the cottage garden is its generosity, its wealth of colour and scent.

Italian gardens

The land of Italy is famous for its beautiful formal gardens, many of which date from the great days of the Italian Renaissance. In everything they did the Italians of the Renaissance, the painters and poets, the architects and garden designers, tried to recreate the glory and the grandeur of ancient Rome. They built new palaces on or near the sites of ancient Roman villas, and in designing the gardens to go with

Left *Piccolomini, garden with fountain,*
above *the garden of the Villa Medici*, right *the plan of Villa d'Este*

the new buildings they adopted the ideals and followed the models of the ancient Romans.

They, too, included statues, fountains and fishponds in their gardens, so that the beauty of stone and the sound of water refreshed the spirits of those who walked along the paths in the green shade of the trees and bushes. As in ancient Roman days the plants and trees came from Nature, but essentially every garden was man-made, everything was given its place by man, for the basic aim of the Italian garden designer was to create order and balance.

He treated the ground like the paper for a painting. First he fixed on a simple rectangular figure, usually a square or rectangle, and then arranged everything inside it according to a well-thought out plan. Paths crossed at right angles, flowers and herbs grew in neat circular beds.

Fountains and statues were placed at fixed points where they could be seen to the best advantage. Bushes were kept thick and low by regular cutting, while rows of trees were grown to shade the walker from the hot Italian sun.

In the picture of the Villa Medici, built in the sixteenth century, there is a garden that has been kept close to the original design. Here can be seen the balance between building, open space and garden, the contrast of light and shade, of low bush and tall tree. Paths are laid, trees and bushes are planted, in geometric order. There is a charming little statue at the centre of the round pond, and everywhere there is a feeling of order and calm. Gardens such as these have stood the test of time, and give visitors as much pleasure today as they gave their original owners centuries ago.

Japanese gardens

No garden lover can fail to be fascinated by the gardens of Japan, so different from anything in the European tradition. The Japanese gardening ideal is not an arrangement of flowers and plants, formal or informal, but the creation of a miniature landscape in which the designer's view of nature is expressed in a small space on a small scale. Art is hidden by art. Trees and bushes, rocks and ponds, little singing streams winding round tiny islands refresh the spirit with their gentle naturalness, but they have all been carefully positioned by the landscape garden designer. Often a tea pavilion, as in the picture, is a graceful part of the scene, and here the ancient Japanese tea ceremony may still be held. Traditionally, to view the moon from a tea pavilion will bring you a sense of peace and well-being, or even the ability to write poetry.

Japanese gardens are full of ancient tradition and symbolic meaning, and many date back as far as AD 600. Streams run from east to west because east is the source of purity and west of impurity. Turtles symbolise long life, so a turtle-shaped rock is always popular. A pine tree twisted in the shape of a crane, a bird that mates for life, represents good luck and lasting companionship. The golden chrysanthemum, sacred symbol of the Imperial family, is cultivated in many shades and forms. The delicate blossom of the cherry tree symbolises the speed with which life fades, while the cherry fruit stands for loyalty. And a cherry blossom party in the Spring is a very lively occasion!

Many gardens seem very simple, but the silver sand is always carefully raked, the ponds in which the goldfish twist and flash are kept perfectly clean, every tree and bush is patiently cut to shape. Plants with different shapes and shades of foliage are placed where they will give the most beautiful effect, and everything is related to the pavilion, for the Japanese garden designer sees house and garden as one beautiful whole. He is a master of nature because he loves the mastery of nature.

NOTES

workhouse house where (in the past) homeless poor people could live but had to work
foliage leaves
blossom (of a fruit tree) have flowers
Renaissance rebirth of learning and the arts in Europe in the fourteenth to sixteenth centuries
herb plant used in cooking or for show

fascinate catch and hold the attention
miniature on a very small scale
symbol an object which represents an idea
AD 600 in the year 600 after the birth of Christ
turtle sea animal with its body protected by a shell into which it can draw its head, tail and legs
crane a bird with long neck and legs
mate make a pair—male and female

EXERCISES

Comprehension

Choose the best answer in each of the following.

1 Italian gardens contain statues, fountains and fishponds similar to those in *a* English cottage gardens; *b* Japanese gardens; *c* ancient Roman gardens; *d* public gardens.

2 Early English cottage gardens were *a* planned by garden designers; *b* not carefully planned; *c* very formal; *d* full of symbolic meaning.

3 Japanese gardens *a* follow the European tradition; *b* are a recent development; *c* are quite unlike European gardens; *d* have been influenced by European gardens.

4 Italian gardens are *a* untidy but beautiful; *b* carefully designed; *c* miniature landscapes; *d* informal.

5 Early English cottage gardens contained *a* only flowers that had been carefully chosen; *b* no vegetables; *c* only self-sown flowers; *d* flowers from many different sources.

Use of English

Combine the following pairs using *so that* and making any necessary changes in tense.

Example We are buying a new house. My parents/can live with us.

Answer We are buying a new house so that my parents can live with us.

Example They moved into the town. The wife/will not need/a car.

Answer They moved into the town so that the wife would not need a car.

1 He planted lots of vegetables. His wife/will not need/buy any.

2 The gardener cut the grass. The club members/can start/their game.

3 A tea pavilion is often built in a Japanese garden. The tea ceremony/can be enjoyed/in beautiful surroundings.

4 We planted scented flowers near the house. Our guests/can smell/them.

5 They moved to a house with a garden. The children/have/somewhere to play.

6 He designed the garden. The owners/have shade/from the sun.

7 Cuttings were given to neighbours. The new varieties/be enjoyed/by many.

8 The Romans included fountains in their gardens. The sound of water/refresh their spirits.

9 He made a slope in the garden. His elderly mother/do some gardening.

10 I have planted my favourite flower in your garden. You/remember/me always.

Guided composition

Write a paragraph describing one of the gardens illustrated in this unit. These questions may help you.

1 Is this garden formal or informal? Has it been carefully designed?

2 Are there flowers, trees, bushes, in the garden? Where are they?

3 Are there paths, fountains, ponds or other constructions in the gardens? Where? Why have they been put there?

4 Is there much contrast in the garden? If not, say what other attraction the garden has.

5 Would you like to spend a lot of time there? Why/Why not?

Vocabulary

Complete this passage by putting the words in brackets in a suitable form.

Japanese Gardens
Streams run from east to west because the east is the source of 1 (*pure*) and the west of 2 (*pure*). Turtles 3 (*symbol*) long life. A tree in the shape of a crane represents good luck and 4 (*companion*). A golden chrysanthemum stands for the 5 (*empire*) Family. The cherry fruit represents 6 (*loyal*).

Discussion

Which of the gardens shown do you like best? Why?

Is a garden 'the purest of human pleasures'?

What are the pleasures in your life?

Does your future lie in the stars?

It has its problems—you can't get all that close to your subject matter for one thing—but astronomy is a fascinating study and its fascination only increases with the perfection of new and more powerful telescopes. Dr Bruce of Edinburgh University discusses the modern situation in this most ancient of sciences.

'I am often asked if a future astronomer should study astronomy, or physics and mathematics at university. The first question I try to settle is "How serious about the subject is our future astronomer?" The mere fact that a student has spent most of his spare time from the age of seven gazing at the stars and building a telescope does not mean that after due attendance at university he'll become an astronomer. Gazing at the stars fascinates all sorts of people. What an astronomer needs are the same qualities that will make a good physicist or mathematician: i.e. a high level of ability and interest in these subjects.

Only first-class students should take up the study of astronomy, for astronomy today is faced with an intellectual challenge which is the equal of that faced by atomic physics in the 1920s. Modern astronomy is concerned not only with the structure of the universe but with why stars exist at all and what the space between the stars is really like. The finest minds are needed to work on these challenging problems.

My own advice to anyone thinking of an astronomical career is to take that physical science at which he will do best, though if a student is very anxious to study astronomy from the start it is possible to take a course in astronomy at several universities. Graduates who have specialised in astronomy can find careers in the photographic, aerospace and computer industries, as well as in pure astronomy, while graduates in related subjects, such as electronic engineering, can take up astronomy at postgraduate level.

Since astronomy is such a vast subject—it is after all one of the oldest, if not the oldest, of sciences, and has had plenty of time to grow— a certain degree of specialisation is to be expected. There are essentially two kinds of astronomer— the observer or optical astronomer, that is the person who is using telescopes and related equipment, and the theorist, whose main instrument is the computer. Britain has for a long time produced excellent theoretical astronomy and, of course, the radio-astronomy done at Manchester and Cambridge is world-famous. Optical astronomy, on the other hand, has been held back until recently by relatively poor equipment.

With the building of new large aperture telescopes at the Royal Greenwich Observatory, England, and in Australia, as part of the joint Anglo-Australian astronomy project, the very sharp division between observer and theorist will start to break down. There will always, of course, be specialists in the mathematical side of the subject, computing models and proposing new theories, and there will always be people working on the more practical side, specialising in the techniques of observation.

Some people consider career prospects in astronomy are poor, arguing from the obvious fact that astronomy is a small profession, but the position is no worse than in the other physical sciences. Anybody seriously interested in a career in astronomy should fix his thoughts firmly on the exciting prospect of being able to use the new telescopes. These instruments, which are among the most advanced pieces of technology

Right *radio telescopes at Cambridge University*

PROSPECTUS INTRA CAMERAM STELLATAM.

in existence, may produce results which completely change our understanding of the structure of the universe.

Consider what happened in the field of radio-astronomy to a young research student at Cambridge, Jocelyn Bell. She was working under Professor Anthony Hewish, who is especially interested in the radio waves picked up from distant galaxies. He designed and built a new radio telescope which started work in 1967 scanning different parts of the heavens as the earth spins round. The results appear as a series of marks on a paper chart. It was Miss Bell's job to check the 100 feet of chart coming out of the machine every day and to note any radio sources that changed rapidly.

In August that year she noticed something strange, an incoming radio signal which appeared at an odd time and lasted only about half as long as the signals from the radio stars under observation. She drew Professor Hewish's attention to it. They carried on with their work, and when, by the end of September, the new signal had appeared about half a dozen times, the Professor

started to use a much faster recorder. On November 28, using this new instrument, they picked up a series of about half a dozen radio pulses just over a second apart, each one lasting for a mere 40 milliseconds.

This was the first observation of the regular radio pulses which gave pulsars their name. Jocelyn Bell, at the start of her career, had been involved in a major scientific discovery. Professor Hewish, who had been in charge of the whole research project, was awarded the Nobel prize for Physics. The discovery of pulsars is a good example of the challenge and rewards of modern astronomy, and shows that the successful astronomer must possess patience, imagination and the ability to attend to details, as well as a firm theoretical understanding of his subject. For someone with these abilities and the right intellectual training, a career in astronomy offers a fascinating future.'

Above *optical astronomy in the seventeenth century*, above right *Herstmonceux castle and gardens*, below right *the domes of the Royal Greenwich observatory*

Night worker

Stars come out at night, so if you happen to be an optical astronomer night time's the only time you can watch them. Ann Savage arrives at the Royal Greenwich Observatory just as the sun is setting. In spite of its name the Observatory isn't at Greenwich, London, for the street lights there are too bright and the atmosphere too dirty. It's at Herstmonceux, Sussex, set in the grounds of an old castle where the wind whistles through the trees round the ornamental lakes. It's just the place for a little man from Mars to arrive and say, 'Take me to your leader', though, disappointingly, Ann doesn't think much of the chances.

'First thing I do is get into my arctic suit,' she says. 'The temperature has to be the same inside the dome as outside, because otherwise the telescopic lens would mist up and spoil the photographic plates I take all night. Then I open the dome to the sky, position the telescope and work out my programme.'

The programme's important, because stars rise and set like the sun, and without exact timing, can be missed altogether. How does she know where they'll be? 'Well, you wouldn't get anywhere by just swinging the telescope and trying to decide which star was which. They don't have their names on them. Their positions are marked on a map of the heavenly bodies, which is rather like maps of the countries of the world.'

Ann is one of a team working on a seven-year-old programme to determine the nature of quasars. No one's quite sure what they are. They have a star-like appearance, but change their light-output in such an unstarlike way they have everyone puzzled. Some quasars change their light output in a day: some in a month, some in a year—and it's Ann's job to keep a check on their behaviour by taking photographs at regular intervals.

It's an exciting and demanding branch of astronomy, but the night-to-night duties can be hard and cheerless. Ann has to work alone and in the dark. 'You get used to the dark and see by the light of the sky. It's the night watchman doing his rounds who knocks into everything and frightens the life out of me.' She has to work in the bitter cold. 'I have to eat sandwiches all night to keep warm.' And she has to work fairly continuously too. 'Some plates need changing every three minutes—there's no chance of a break. But sometimes I have a one-hour exposure—then there's time to hurry over to the rest room and make a cup of coffee.'

Doesn't she ever get lonely, with nothing but the dark around her, and the never-ending universe above her? 'Not really. There are six other telescopes and I know there are people working them even if I can't call across to them.' Well, doesn't her husband get lonely? 'He's fairly used to it. Usually he says, "Good, I'll go all-night fishing." I suppose there are things I hate about the night shift, especially when it starts cloudy, clears around 3 am, but by the time I've driven to work and opened up the dome— it's clouded over again. On the whole, though, the work's very rewarding. You feel wonderful driving home with the sunrise. Everywhere's fresh; the rabbits are out playing, the milkman's just starting his rounds. You really feel you've done something worthwhile.'

NOTES
challenge call to fight
graduate one who has successfully completed university; *postgraduate*—continuing to study after becoming a graduate
vast very great
aperture opening
prospect what is to be expected
galaxy very large system of stars

scan observe systematically
pulse sudden, quickly passing, increase of power
lens shaped glass to make an object appear less distant
which star was which which star one was looking at
at regular intervals an equal time apart
do (his) rounds do (his) duty by visiting every part of (the observatory) regularly
exposure leaving the camera lens open
night shift turn to work at night

EXERCISES

Comprehension

Imagine you are a careers officer and answer these questions from a school leaver interested in a career in astronomy.

1 What qualities does an astronomer need?
2 Why do you think it is a difficult science to study?
3 Which physical science should I study if I want to be an astronomer?
4 What career opportunities are there for someone who has studied astronomy?
5 Do all astronomers do the same kind of work?
6 What type of work is being done in Britain?
7 Why do some people say career prospects in astronomy are poor?
8 Why do you say a career in astronomy could be very exciting in the future.

Use of English *to get used to —ing*

Example I didn't like working outside London. Now I don't mind.
Answer I have got used to working outside London.
Example At first I hated working unusual hours. I stopped minding about it last year.
Answer I got used to working unusual hours last year.
Rewrite the following.

1 At first the young man hated working alone. Now he doesn't mind.
2 He didn't enjoy starting work at sunset. He stopped minding it last summer.
3 He is frightened when he hears noises in the night. Soon he will not be frightened by them.
4 He didn't like feeling cold all night. He's beginning not to mind.
5 He hated arriving at work to find the sky cloudy. He still hates it.
6 At first his wife complained about being alone at night. Now she doesn't mind.

Guided writing

The careers officer has arranged for the school leaver to meet Ann Savage. Write the questions that Ann answers in this dialogue.
Student:
Ann: The street lighting was too bright and the atmosphere too dirty.
Student:
Ann: I start working at sunset and work until sunrise.
Student:
Ann: I got used to it. It's lovely driving home in the early morning.
Student:
Ann: The one thing I don't like is feeling cold all night.
Student:
Ann: Not often. Only when the night watchman makes a noise.
Student:
Ann: I'm studying quasars.
Student:
Ann: I take photos of them at regular intervals.
Student:
Ann: Yes, I do. On the whole it's very rewarding.

Vocabulary

Complete the following by putting the words in brackets in a suitable form.
Astronomy has always been a 1 (*fascinate*) subject and the new 2 (*power*) telescopes make it even more 3 (*excite*). An astronomer needs the same qualities as a good 4 (*physics*) or 5 (*mathematics*) i.e. a high level of 6 (*able*) in these subjects.

Discussion

What are the problems of people who work at night?
Do you think the study of astronomy is important? Why?

ACKNOWLEDGEMENTS

We are grateful to the following for permission to reproduce copyright photographs and illustrations material:

Aerofilms Ltd., page 93; Michael Andrews page 5; Ove Arup Partnership page 6; Barnaby's Picture Library pages 24 and 73; British Film Institute, Roy Export Company Establishment Copyright, page 42 and for the following Charlie Chaplin Films: page 42, The Goldrush page 43(left), The Circus page 43(right), Modern Times page 44; Brooke Bond Liebig Ltd., page 21(left); Cadbury Typhoo Food Advisory Service (Cadburys Soya Choice) page 39(top); Camera Press Ltd., pages 14, 30, 31 and 51; Cavendish Laboratory, University of Cambridge page 91; Central Press Ltd., page 46; Colorific pages 13 and 80; Department of Energy, Crown Copyright reproduced by permission of the Controller, HM Stationery Office page 35; Dr P.G. Harris, Open University page 76; FAO page 39 (bottom); John Hedgecoe page 64 (top); Japan National Tourist Organisation page 88; Keystone Press Agency Ltd; page 47; Mansell Collection page 21 (bottom right); Henry Moore pages 62, 63, 64 (bottom), 65, 66; Nobel Foundation page 81; Open University page 56; Oxfam page 12 (photo by Nick Fogden); Picturepoint Ltd., page 4; Punch Publications page 60 (bottom); Radio Times Hulton Picture Library pages 21 (top right) and 87; Reginald Davis FIIP., FRPS., pages 28, 29 and 32; Reportagebild, Sweden page 82 (top); Science Museum pages 25 and 92; Harry Sowden page 7; The Clockmakers Company, Guildhall Library page 26; Thames and Hudson, Georgina Masson Copyright page 86; Transworld Feature Syndicate Inc., page 77 (photo by Cheze Brown); Valerie Finnis pages 84 and 85; WHICH Magazine page 50.

The illustrations are by Joseph Wright pages 16 and 17; Graham Round pages 20 and 72; Sara Silcock pages 22 and 48; Shirley Parfitt page 36; Malcolm Bird page 40; Malcolm Booker pages 68 and 70.

The cover shows a detail from Three Rings (1966) by Henry Moore.

We are grateful to the following for permission to reproduce or adapt copyright material:

Michael Joseph Ltd and Simon and Schuster Inc for abridged extracts and stories from Particularly Cats by Doris Lessing copyright © 1967 by Doris Lessing Productions Ltd; author's agent and Scott Meredith Literary Agency Inc for an extract from 'Essays on Dogs' by P.G. Wodehouse in Son Of A Bitch by Elliot Erwitt reprinted by permission of the author's estate and the author's agents; the author for extracts from his article in Woman's Own 25th January, 1975 by William Hamilton MP; Syndication International Ltd for an adapted article 'Love Is Where You Find It' in Woman's Own June 7, 1975; the author for his article on Antiques by Tony Curtis in Ideal Home Magazine; The Australian Government Publishing Service for extracts from an Australian Government Publication on 'The Sydney Opera House'; The Nobel Foundation for extracts from their brochure 'Alfred Nobel and the Nobel Prizes'; Over 21 Magazine for extracts from the article 'Night People' from Over 21 December 1973, reproduced by permission; the author for extracts from Don't Just Sit There by Miss M. Perigoe; The New Internationalist for an article from The New Internationalist March 1975; Education Unit Voluntary Committee on Overseas Aid and Development for a factsheet adapted from 'Facts about Development 1: Population' published by the Voluntary Committee on Overseas Aid and Development.